Joy To the World

Christmas Carols made new for the 21ˢᵗ century

Diarmuid O'Murchu MSC

Copyright © Diarmuid O'Murchu, 2024

All rights reserved. No part of this publication may be reproduced, stored or transmitted in any form by any means, electronic, mechanical, photocopying or otherwise, without the prior written permission of the publisher or author.

First published in Great Britain in 2024 by Sleepy Lion Publishing. (Trading name of Sleepy Lion Limited)

Text Copyright © Diarmuid O'Murchu, 2024
Cover © Sleepy Lion Publishing 2024
Interior art © Sleepy Lion Publishing, 2024
Editing © Sleepy Lion Publishing, 2024

The right of to be identified as author of this work has been asserted in accordance with the Copyright, Designs and Patents Act, 1988.

ISBN: 978-1-917563-01-7

www.sleepylionpublishing.com

Dedication

To Mothers and Midwives

Birthing forth new life

in those parts of our world

where the violence of war and oppression

deliver death rather than new life.

Acknowledgements

As an author of over 30 books, many informed by so many inspiring sources, I have long acknowledged the wisdom which my books embody. On this occasion my gratitude moves in a different direction, including a special thanks to Michael Amos, my editor at Sleepy Lion Publishing.

For me, Christmas has always been very special, myself born on December 23rd into a poor rural community where the simple joys of home and family embody a creative impulse that defies rational explanation. For those who lit the Christmas candles, baked the Christmas cake, went to Church before the dawn even broke, for the magic of Santa, and the sheer joy of being alive, I have always given thanks, and I always will.

For those who birthed all such possibilities, and for those who over many years became soulmates in the transition from childhood to old age, you are a sacred memory forever inscribed in my heart. As you have blessed me, so I bless you too, with deep love and gratitude. Amen!

Contents

Introduction _____ 1

Part One: What Makes Christmas Carols so Special? _____ 5

Chapter One: Sacred Songs of Deep Archetypal Meaning _____ 8

Chapter Two: Songs of Cosmic and Planetary Resonance ____ 16

Chapter Three: Carols Proclaiming the Power of Birthing ____ 26

Chapter Four: Rebirthing the Inner Child — beyond unprocessed chilhood fear _____ 35

Chapter Five: Birthing in the Power of Womanhood _____ 43

Part Two: Carols in a New Language for the 21st Century ____ 59

Chapter One: Carols for Everyone, Christian or Otherwise ___ 62

Chapter Two: It is time to Outgrow the Imperial Language ___ 70

Chapter Three: Decolonising the Christmas Carols _____ 81

Chapter Four: Music of the Spheres: Even Creation Sings ____ 92

Chapter Five: The Wisdom of Archetypes, Our Hidden Resource _____ 102

References _____ 116

Introduction

Language shapes our ability to imagine the possibilities inherent in our world. Paul Levy.

For one month every year, the Christian world exults in joyous praise. Christmas Carols break free from church buildings and from religious choirs. They spill on to our streets, shopping malls, and market squares. The air is filled with a sense of jubilation. And so many people, some with much faith, some with little or none, all join in the melodious rapture.

What is it about that rapture that is so appealing to so many people? There is something deeply alluring about many of those melodies. They are like subliminal waves of energy that carry us along, lifting our spirits and reinvigorating our hearts. They touch some deep inner core. They awaken new levels of meaning.

This illusive underlying feature is what I describe as the *archetypal*, a much neglected feature of the human search for meaning, one that is often confused with religion, but in fact it predates religion by many thousands of years. To appreciate and understand more fully this archetypal power, we need to rescue the Christmas Carols from their often narrow religious language, one that is quite outdated and to many people feels irrelevant.

For a growing body of religious people as well, the language feels irrelevant and even archaic Moreover, in the light of current theological awareness, such religious language is not even good theology, as theology and scripture seek to outgrow a three-tier cosmology, with its imperial God-imagery, and a spirituality largely focused on human sin and depravity.

In this small book, I offer another set of words for many of the best-known Christmas Carols. I want to bring the language into tune with the archetypal power of the melodious music. Archetypes stretch our sense of meaning: they tend to enlarge our worldview and open us up to the deeper meaning of our existence — individually and collectively. Let's opt for the kind of language that will support and enhance that expanded view of life.

Therefore, it is the language of the Carols I want to change, not the music, nor the popular melodies. As I have already indicated, the melodious tenor is the medium that carries the archetypal energy, which is the reason why so many people warm to the melodies and spontaneously sing along. But let's start using words that support that same creative energy. It will make the experience of the Carol-singing all the more enriching.

Part One

What Makes Christmas Carols so Special?

All over the world, in Christian lands and elsewhere, Christmas marks a celebration unique for its joviality, comradery, and lightness of being. Often described as a season of goodwill, it draws together people of diverse cultures and values. Even among those of little or no religion, a sense of spirituality exudes, particularly as people join in singing carols for a range of supportive causes or simply to participate in the common mood of celebration.

Behind, or perhaps beneath, the flurry of excitement one detects a creative energy that transcends human reason and defies human explanation. I describe it as an *archetypal force*, the meaning of which I will introduce in Chapter One, with further elaboration throughout the book.

The archetypal context I adopt stretches us beyond the conventional understanding of faith, whether in Christianity or indeed in any of the major world religions. We are being invited into enlarged horizons of meaning, with an expanded vision of cosmic and planetary proportion.

Much of the attention of Part One of this book is devoted to the metaphor of Birthing, described in the Gospels as if it is a form of divine creation totally beyond human or earthly possibility. When re-examined within an archetypal context, it becomes a creative possibility not merely for all humans, but for every evolutionary breakthrough that has happened throughout the entire story the creation we inhabit. Within that novel focus on fertile birthing, the role of womanhood, personally, and metaphorically, takes on a radically new meaning, a reawakening of the feminine not merely within women, but within all organic life-forms.

In addressing the Christian context, particularly the infancy narratives of Matthew and Luke, I give particular attention to what contemporary scholars name as "reworking the tradition." In the popular Christian context, we tend to focus on the coming of Jesus into our world 2,000 years ago, to bring about the redemption and salvation of sinful humans. But that is a very narrow meaning of tradition, and one that is becoming less credible or intelligible even for many people who still identify as Christian.

All of this requires us to explore another way of wording the Christmas Carols, a new language that will also illuminate a new way of understanding Jesus, throwing up new challenges for how Christians are called to live their faith in our modern world. And surprisingly, as we come to this fresh understanding of the Christian faith, we encounter an adult appropriation that will be of interest to a range of other people, even those who don't follow any one formal religion.

Chapter One

Sacred Songs of Deep Archetypal Meaning

Archetypes are shared patterns of human sense-making and behaviour that are deeply meaningful and universal to human experience. Jeremy Lent.

Wherever we are at Christmas time, we can hear the carols resounding: it is the most wonderful time of the year. Although of religious significance for Christians only, people all over the world enter the spirit of joviality. Families gather from diverse places, gifts are exchanged, while food and drink are consumed amid an air of celebration.

Among Christians, one detects a nostalgic sense of a much-loved devotion that has lost much of its fervour in our time. It might be the only day of the year in which some Christians go to Church, yet it feels important to fulfil that much of a religious duty. And alongside the tinsel, the Christmas tree, and the often elaborate range of decorations, the Christmas crib still retains a prominent place.

Many claim that Christmas is now so commercialised that it has lost virtually all religious meaning. One wonders if Christmas is a religious feast that has given pride of place to extensive shopping and retail therapy, or an occasion with a subverted sublimity waiting to be rediscovered. I opt for the latter.

According to traditional belief, Christmas marks the divine prerogative whereby God sent his beloved son, Jesus, for the salvation of humankind. According to the doctrine of the *Incarnation* (coming in the flesh) the divine Son of God takes on human flesh and becomes one of us. Allegedly, this never happened before and will never happen again. Jesus is purported to be the one and only Saviour for all humankind.

God's coming in our flesh is described in the Gospels of Matthew and Luke as a miraculous event, a conception made possible by the special intervention of the Holy Spirit, bypassing normal human intercourse. The intention seems to be that the all holy, pure God can only enter our sin-infested world by a divinely instituted arrangement. God incarnates in and through human flesh, but only by a special arrangement in which the power of the divine clearly supersedes that of the human.

Over the centuries, millions have drawn comfort and consolation from this divine reassurance, while the Christian Church has often used the doctrine of the incarnation to assert its supremacy over all other beliefs, whether Christian or otherwise. While the feast of Christmas still continues to evoke devotion and hope for those who are impoverished or marginalized, theologically it raises a range of questions requiring a much more discerning response.

Archetypes and the human search for meaning

As I've stated previously, for many people, religious or not, Christian or otherwise, Christmas is marked by the singing of carols and the playing of carol music. The melodies carry a deep inexplicable resonance with an appeal far beyond the religious and Christian significance. People from all over the world can be heard humming or chanting the melodies, rehearsing them internally, with or without words. This deep resonance is what psychologists name as the *archetypal*. There is more to these memorable melodies than just religious hymns of the Christmas season.

Archetypes have been adopted by both anthropology and psychology, and more recently in cosmology-based studies, to name and explain those sublime energetic forces that transcend our rational and common-sense modes of understanding. Consequently, all human aspiration, desire, and action arise from the energetic creativity of archetypes. Moreover, all archetypal truth is spiritual in nature, often transcending the doctrines and structures of the formal religions and forever luring us into a deeper search for meaning. Jungian theorist James Hillman claims that archetypal psychology is theophonic, describing the inmost soul — not necessarily the deities of formal religions — that grounds everything in the realm of deep meaning. (More in Hillman 1975; 1983).

Archetypes invite us into a deeper way of seeing and understanding life. Religious people might describe it as a more contemplative way, long associated with a form of religious experience known as mysticism. Before pursuing such lofty spiritual heights, we can access the archetypal in a range of ordinary life experiences. I find it helpful to distinguish between instincts and archetypes. For instance we have heard stories of children in institutional settings (e.g., boarding schools) who eat far more food than they would consume at home; in other words food is being consumed as a psychological compensation for the lack of homely love and care. The hunger for food (instinct) is more to the fore because the sharing of food that creates love and intimacy (archetype) is lacking. The archetype serves deeper internal values.

Many people have the experience of desiring what others

have and, as a result, often feel jealousy or even resentment. In psychological language, we project onto others some of our unmet needs. The felt emotions of jealousy or resentment denote the instinct. The needs that are not being met belong to the realm of the archetype. To identify such needs and seek their fulfilment is not selfishness, but an important task of growing more fully into our deeper human selves.

A final example is from the realm of human sexuality. Sex is popularly portrayed as a means for human procreation, a Darwinian drive (instinct) for the perpetuation of the species. But human sexuality is about a great deal more than biological reproduction. It is primarily about the love and intimacy that humans desire to share. That is the sexual archetype, sometimes described as a capacity and desire for deep bonding. A great deal of sexual acting-out (and abuse) in the modern world arises from a raw hunger (instinctual) for a level of human intimacy (the archetype) made ever more difficult in a culture of much sexual confusion.

The archetypal dimension of the Christmas Carols

Many of the Christmas Carols carry archetypal meaning, not in their words or conceptual ideas, but by the power of melody and music. Often the words and the theological concepts distract from, and even undermine, this deeper layer of meaning. I propose, therefore, that we attempt a realignment of word and melody, that we adopt words and expressions that stand a better chance of honouring the deeper meaning that engages us in the allurement of the carols. Basically, the deep underlying meaning is compromised by some or all of the following factors:

1. The popular Christmas story (based mainly on the early chapters of the Gospels of Matthew and Luke), is narrowly anthropocentric. Only human beings — and their salvation — matters. The archetypal dimensions embrace wider transpersonal and even cosmic dimensions, opening up aspirations and hopes not merely for human meaning but creating new possibilities for how we see and understand creation at large.

2. Universally, we witness a tendency to rationalize and literalize the Gospel-inherited story of Jesus, usually portrayed to be rational, historical fact, when in truth it has little or nothing to do with factual history. Most of the story is midrash, in which older material (from the Hebrew Scriptures) is retold to make sense of present events. (More in Keenan 2021). The Christmas story carries levels of meaning much bigger than the formal religion being represented.

3. The focus is largely on Jesus as an individualized person, a divine-human being, employing an understanding of personhood that belongs to classical Greek anthropology, and therefore it fails to honour our true evolutionary story of some seven million years.

4. With Jesus portrayed as God incarnate among us (God

coming in human flesh) we witness a splitting of the sacred and the secular that belongs largely to the dominant Greek culture of the time of Jesus, undermining the integration of both the human and the divine in the wider transpersonal sphere.

5. Many of the Carols, and Bible-based readings used at Christmas, portray Jesus as an eminently imperial figurehead, representing the God who rules from above the sky through earthly kings. This divine imperialism is an inheritance of Roman imperial theology and needs to be removed entirely from the Christian story. (More in Crossan 2007; 2022).

6. The focus on God as a vulnerable child begets a strong sense of devotional faith, often inhibiting and undermining the quality of adult identity and integrity necessary to understand and appropriate the archetypal intent of the Christmas message.

7. Many Carols belong to a distinctly, even exclusive, Western (European) context, focussing on short days, cold weather, European lifestyle and value, whereas archetypal values are innately universal in nature and impact. We need a version of the carols that will inspire and empower people across the human population.

While acknowledging that the Carols in their current format carry a great deal of meaning for people of more devotional faith, and particularly for the millions in our world condemned to poverty, marginalization, and dislocation, which is why we need to rescue these melodies from their limited religious context. We want another version, one that will honour the capacity of the carols to inspire and empower everybody, poor and rich alike.

The Christmas Carols carry the potential for a great deal of cultural transformation and spiritual empowerment. For many, they carry cherished memories, but, more importantly deeper aspirations, which are felt and imagined and often not capable of being explained in conventional human language. The carols lift our minds and spirits to loftier heights, where the mystery of life — in ourselves and in all creation — becomes ever more radiant and inspiring.

Chapter Two

Songs of Cosmic and Planetary Resonance

In every cubic inch, anywhere in the entire universe, protons and other elementary particles are sprouting forth. A realm of infinite generativity. Brian Swimme.

From the time of his birth, and for some 30 years that followed, the story of Jesus is about *one* person, who lived two thousand years ago on one tiny planet rotating around *one* star out of hundreds of billions of stars in the Milky Way galaxy, itself, *one* out of a trillion galaxies. The immensity of all this might seem to make Jesus' life (and ours) utterly insignificant. That is what happens when religious focus is too small and our understanding of creation doesn't go beyond the Genesis story. But, if we believe that the *Spirit of God* was present from the very beginning, 14 billion years ago, the immensity only fills us with awe, wonder, and reassurance.

The inherited story of the Christ child, born to Jewish parents in the earthly setting of Bethlehem of Judea, has been cast into a historical legend that subverts and even undermines the archetypal significance, briefly reviewed in Chapter One. In time, the story became that of salvation for sinful humans, when in fact it really describes the power of embodied love radiating throughout the entire creation.

What do we mean by Christ?

This is how the Franciscan spiritual writer, Richard Rohr, seeks to reclaim the deeper, enlarged meaning of Christian faith for our time:

> Our faith became a competitive theology, with various parochial theories of salvation, instead of a universal cosmology inside of which all can live with an inherent dignity... Christ is God, and Jesus is Christ's historical manifestation in time... Instead of saying that God came into the world through Jesus, maybe it would be better to say that Jesus came out of an already Christ-soaked world... Until we start reading the Jesus story through the collective notion that the Christ offers us, I honestly think we miss

much of the core message, and read it all in terms of individual salvation, and individual reward and punishment. (Rohr, 2019, pp 15, 17, 18, 163).

When we hear the words *Jesus Christ*, we can easily identify Christ as Jesus' surname. People of a more scholarly ilk will know that "Christ" means *Messia*h, denoting the Anointed One from God. Adopting the archetypal slant, Rohr contends that Christ means the universality of God, the God of the entire creation, while Jesus references the unique historical person of 2,000 years ago.

Accordingly, the Christ is the creative God pre-existing in time and sustaining all life past, present and future. Hence Rohr's term "a Christ-soaked world," out of which come galaxies and stars, planets and all sentient beings, including Jesus of Nazareth. And Jesus, like all other life forms, lives inside a universal cosmology, which in Gospel terms is described as the Kingdom of God. one of the most misunderstood terms in the Christian faith.

Jesus and the New Reign of God

Frequently throughout the synoptic Gospels (Matthew, Mark, and Luke) Jesus describes his mission using the phras*e: the Kingdom of God.* Poorly understood in the New Testament, this phrase has been grossly distorted throughout much of Christian history. For some thousands of years before the emergence of

Christianity, the king was regarded as God's primary representative on earth, not merely in the Hebrew Scriptures (O.T.) but for long before that epoch.

Not surprising, therefore, we see the Gospel writers, Matthew and Luke, portraying Jesus as a royal patriarchal person, whose ancestry goes right back to King David. There is little or no historical evidence for these genealogies (Matt. 1:1-17; Lk. 3:23-38). They were intended to be read (or heard) as proof for the divinity of Jesus, understood to be a legacy inherited from the God who rules from above the sky and mediates the power of such divinity primarily through royal lines of descent.

But how concerned was Jesus about his divinity? And how did he regard the royal entourage upon which his authenticity as a Godlike Messiah was postulated?

Prior to the time of the Roman Emperor, Constantine (early 4th century), this royal status of Jesus seems to have meant very little among the early Christians (cf. Vearncombe, 2022), and since the mid 20th century, it became an ever more questionable feature in the scholarly understanding of Jesus. Most disturbing of all is the growing realisation that the historical Jesus himself seems to have had little interest in such royal accolade, and, much more seriously, seems to have rejected it completely.

All of this brings us back to the phrase: *the Kingdom of God*. What did it actually mean for Jesus? It seems to have been the cryptic statement in which Jesus was proclaiming "a new reign of God" radically at variance with the inherited religious tradition around which kingship was construed. It seems to have been focussed on empowerment rather than patriarchal power — hence the translation I use in all my books: *the Companionship of Empowerment*.[1] And most revolutionary of all, it was not a strategy for human salvation, either in this world or in the next, but an empowering, egalitarian vision that included the whole spectrum of creation from the vast cosmos to the tiny sub-atomic particles.

The Jesuit theologian, Roger Haight, offers this cryptic resume:

> The rule of God refers to the intention of the Creator, the way God desires creation to be, especially human existence in a community that includes relationship with the wider life of the planet... The rule of God represents no small insight. It symbolizes being drawn into the mystery of God's intention for the universe... It opens up a framework of how human beings should live and what they should live for in this world. (Haight 2019, 214).

---

[1] This phrase was originally used by Scripture scholar, John Dominic Crossan, suggesting how the people would have heard the phrase Kingdom of God, in the original Aramaic in which Jesus would have spoken and preached. (More in O'Murchu 2017, 114ff)

The enlarged cosmic/planetary horizon is made even more explicit by the theologian, Elizabeth Johnson:

> Since the reign of God is especially attentive to the needy and outcast, Jesus showed a partisanship for suffering people that we can today interpret as extending to encompass the earth and its myriads of distressed species and ecosystems. His ministry reveals a wideness in God's mercy that includes all creation. (Johnson, 2020, 82).

Over the centuries, Christians sought to prioritise a personal relationship with God and Jesus, exalting human personhood over all other lifeforms. This anthropocentric view of our humanity (only humans matter) is proving to be a major threat to our very survival on this earth. More importantly, we now better understand its significance as a cultural construct we projected onto God (himself), validating human supremacy over all other life forms.

And we have long assumed that this is also the way in which Jesus understood life, purporting a mission largely if not totally for humans only. But the new reign of God (the new companionship) is a trans-human vision, embracing the entire creation. And only in the context of such an enlarged vision can humans hope to realise their God-given potentials. In contemporary terms, without a meaningful earth and cosmos we humans, will not enjoy a life of meaning and purpose.

Carols honouring the New Reign of God

Two strands have been highlighted in this Chapter. First, Jesus as the Christ is not about imperial Messiahship, but denotes something of God's unconditional love for the entire creation. Secondly, Jesus belongs to that same creation-centred context and proclaimed that enlarged vision in the Gospel strategy of the New Reign of God.

How, then, does our celebration of Christmas honor and promote that enlarged vision? And how might the Christmas Carols honor and proclaim that sense of global liberation and empowerment?

Some researchers trace the Carols back to pagan songs sung at various celebrations of the winter solstice, as people danced around stone circles. The word *carol* comes from the old French word 'carole', which meant a popular circle dance accompanied by singing. The ancient Roman pagan festival of Saturnalia, which honoured the agricultural god Saturn, took place near the winter solstice. Many of the traditions we now associate with Christmas, such as wreaths, candles, feasting, gift-giving, song, and music can be traced back to the celebration of Saturnalia. It was only later that carols began to be sung in church and to be specifically associated with Christmas.

From within those pagan origins, we can reclaim the love for nature and an encounter with holy mystery in the midst of creation, even amid the darkness and difficulties of wintertime. Today, of course, we must remember that most practising Christians (regular Church-goers) live in the southern hemisphere, amid weather conditions often quite different from the winter-conditions traditionally associated with our celebration of Christmas. Adjustments need to be made so that all Christians are included, keeping in mind that radical inclusivity is a central feature of the New Reign of God.

It is that broader spiritual vision known to our ancient ancestors we now need to retrieve and reclaim. This is not merely a nostalgia for a long-lost idyllic past, but an emergence of our time in the 21st century with a strong and urgent relevance for a world in peril, for a secular sacredness that has been suppressed to the detriment not merely of human beings, but to that of all the other creatures who share the web of life with us.

Wisdom of the Parable

In their overview of Christmas and its biblical meaning, scripture scholars Marcus Borg and John Dominic Crossan suggest that we approach the various aspects of the Christmas story as *parabolic overtures* (Borg & Crossan 2007, 38ff). In other words, don't succumb to literal interpretation. Christians will be familiar with the Gospel notion of Jesus speaking in parables, the key features of which may be synthesised as follows:

- Parables as told by Jesus have a distinctive subversive flavour with few precedents in ancient Hebrew literature. These are stories that challenge and disturb several sanctioned cultural and moral norms.
- Parables stretch conventional wisdom to breaking point and beyond.
- Parables leave the hearer with dislocated feelings and major conceptual adjustments.
- Parables resolve nothing; rather they open up reality into a vast new range of fresh possibilities.
- All the parables require inclusiveness of previously excluded dimensions of life.
- The parables break through the dualistic split between the sacred and the secular. (More in O'Murchu 2019, 132ff).

By adding the word 'overtures', Borg and Crossan invite us into that receptive disposition, the curious anticipation of deeper wisdom. In other words, a readiness for what the French philosopher, Paul Riceour calls *a surplus of meaning*, always stretching us beyond literal understandings.

All of this is not merely about the religious domain and the radical new horizons into which Jesus was (and is) inviting Christian followers, but rather the archetypal realm of value and meaning, which stretches us beyond the personal and interpersonal, into the expansive horizons of the creation we inhabit. This wider horizon of creation has long been a neglected element in our understanding of the Christian faith, specifically the vision of Jesus encapsulated in the notion of the Kingdom of God, which has tragically been reduced to redemption and salvation for humans only, when, it seems, Jesus envisaged the vision as one embracing the entire web of cosmic and planetary life.

While we enjoy Christmas with family and friends, grateful for the human love that nurtures and sustains us, let us also recall that the gift of life is an endowment rich in cosmic significance, beginning with the carbon from exploded stars, foundational to every form of organic life — we are stardust! We also need to remember that the salt in our sweat and tears, the calcium of our bones, and the iron in our blood all eroded out of the rocks of Earth's crust, and the sulphur of the protein molecules in our hair and muscles was spewed out by volcanoes.

When will we celebrate and proclaim in song (carol) — such a rich and complex endowment? Earthlings adorned with the glory of God radiant throughout all creation!

Chapter Three

Carols Proclaiming the Power of Birthing

What does God do all day long? God lies on a maternity bed giving birth all day long. Meister Eckhart.

When it comes to the Christmas archetypes, that of the Birther takes strong priority. The infant in the Christmas crib signifies a great deal more than just another newly born entering the world. In religious terms it signifies the mighty God entering our world amid vulnerability and fragility. But even for non-religious persons, the imagery evokes a deep feeling touching into subliminal depths that cannot be explained in rational terms.

Christians and followers of other religions have inherited religious traditions in which God tends to be described as Master, Lord, Ruler, Judge, Saviour, King. These titles carry connotations of power, domination, and control. However, when it comes to the metaphor of the *Birther,* one strongly favoured by mystics and feminists, our sense of God changes dramatically.

Contemporary theologians tend to describe Incarnation (God coming in the flesh) in terms of *embodiment*; we might say 'enfleshment'. Theologian Elizabeth Johnson (2020, 183ff) notes that the word used for flesh in the Hebrew Scriptures, namely *basar,* carries quite a different meaning from the term *sarx* used by St. Paul. While *sarx* usually denotes human flesh prone to sin and weakness, *basar* is better translated as *fleshiness* and should be understood as a characteristic of all organic life, of every embodied form we know in creation.

In that case, the God who incarnates in bodies does not begin with the human person, but with the universe at large. In the evolving cosmos of some 14 billion years, God has been incarnating, that is, birthing new life, throughout all that time. The primary body in which God incarnates is not the human being, but the cosmos at large. And God continues to incarnate in every celestial body, in stars, galaxies, planets, the sun, moon, and in our home planet, the Earth, in existence for some 4 billion years.

I now invite the reader to keep two notions close to together: God incarnates by birthing forth a vast range of bodies. *Incarnating* and *birthing* need to be kept closely aligned. No sooner has planet earth been birthed than we begin to see a vast range of life-structures and forms coming into being, right down to the tiny organisms, atoms and cells that constitute the life we see all around us.

The Christian tendency to equate incarnation with humans only is what today we describe as *anthropocentrism*, a conviction of a few thousand years that only humans matter and that everything has been created for the benefit of the human. This view fails to honour the creativity of God, and of the universe, elegantly revealed in all that has been created across the entire web of creation. Worse still, it also undermines what God's intention is for our human species, and this brings us to another problematic horizon of our time, namely anthropology.

Christian theology defines incarnation within the understanding of the human (anthropology) which prevailed about two-thousand years ago when the historical Jesus came on earth. But humans have existed for an estimated *seven million years*, and the creative God has been birthing new possibilities in our species throughout that entire time. The birthing of God in the human species did not begin two-thousand years ago. It began seven million years ago, when we first came into being as God's latest expression of divine birthing.

Why restrict God's creativity to a few recent millennia? Why reduce divine birthing of new life to one special person, who lived merely two thousand years ago? When are we humans going to allow God to be God in all that elegant birthing that belongs to deep time?[2]

1. O Come You Sacred Earthlings (O Come All Ye Faithful)

The earliest printed version of this hymn is in a book published by John Francis Wade (d. 1786), but the earliest manuscript bears the name of the Portuguese, King John IV (d.1656). The English translation of "O Come, All Ye Faithful" was composed in 1841 by an English Catholic priest, Frederick Oakeley. It is a favourite carol often sung at the beginning or end of religious services during the Christmas season.

For our time, we need to expand that sense of faithful calling to include our identity as Earthlings, inviting us to engage more fully in birthing new possibilities for God's creation, and working more collaboratively with the God-ever-with-us, Emmanuel-God, so that together we can bring healing and love to our wounded earth.

---

[2] Here the reader may wish to explore the bold suggestion of the theologian, Catherine Keller, that we should replace the inherited notion of God creating *ex nihilo* (from nothing) to that of God creating *ex profundis* (from the profound depths) (Keller 2003). Quantum physics describes such profound depths as the creative vacuum. (Levy 2018)

O come, all you people, faithful and expectant,

O come you, all singing, this new song of hope.

Come forth with courage, Spirit wise and holy.

REFRAIN: O come, you sacred Earthlings, with healing hope now birthing. O come now and deliver, that all may be free.

Set free from bondage, life from light eternal;

Graceful empowering for all now to see.

God's love has freed us, hearts no longer broken. (Refrain).

Sing we so grateful, love on earth incarnate,

God's presence with us, E-mann–uel!

Transforming justice, birthing forth new freedom. (Refrain).

Come God's own people, on the earth reborn

Renew creation, let all now rejoice.

Fear won't control us, true love all enduring. (Refrain).

2. Let Every Town Give Refuge! (O Little Town of Bethlehem)

On Christmas Eve in 1865, an Episcopal priest, Phillips Brooks (1835–1893), based in Philadelphia (USA), travelled on horseback from Jerusalem to Bethlehem and visited, according to the story, the spot where Jesus was born. Three years later, he wrote the poem for a Christmas Sunday-school service and asked his organist, Lewis Redner, to set it to music. In Louis F. Benson's *Studies of Familiar Hymns*, Redner is quoted as saying: "I was roused from sleep late in the night hearing an angel-strain whispering in my ear, and seizing a piece of music paper I jotted down the treble of the tune as we now have it. Neither Mr. Brooks nor I ever thought the carol or the music to it would live beyond that Christmas of 1868."

Similar to many hymns written in the 1800s, this carol has a strong devotional feel to it, with a specific appeal for children. Moving beyond the devotional sentiment, the carol can also evoke the call to justice, especially for the poor and the marginalised of our world.

O little town of Bethlehem, what destiny you share?
So small and unassuming, till fame your thoroughfare.
The God of dear surprises, inhabiting your space
To graciate humanity and walk our earth in grace.
The silent earth is watching upon this blessed night
And every heart is yearning, our fears are put to flight
The little town will celebrate, invading forces out;
Instead we welcome refugees as all are homeward bound.
Our children safe are sleeping, God watches all this night
The outcast and the sinner, embrace the same twilight.
The pilgrim and sojourner are welcome to our home,
As Earthlings graced abundantly, beneath one skyline dome.

3. Birthing the First Humans (The First Noel)

This carol is of Cornish origin. Its current form was first published in *Carols Ancient and Modern* (1823) and in *Gilbert and Sandys Carols* (1833), both of which were edited by William Sandys and arranged by Davies Gilbert (who also wrote extra lyrics) for *Hymns and Carols of God*.

Nowell is an Early Modern English synonym of "Christmas" from the French *Noël* "the Christmas season", ultimately from the Latin *natalis*, indicating birthing. The word was regularly used in carols dated to the Middle Ages. Noel or Noël has been in use as both a given name and a surname since the 12th century, particularly for children born over the Christmas period.

In its traditional form, this carol carries echoes of origins, not merely about God manifest in the person of Jesus (for the first time), but the God who has been birthing forth in all human life over the time span of our evolutionary story of *seven million years*. Let's hear the carol in the context of that expanded narrative and the birthing forth that ensued across deep time.

> *The first Noel whose birthing declared*
> *of humans evolving from Africa's flare*
> *For over these years, seven million in all*
> *humans birthed new life with a dignified call.*
> *Noel, Noel, Noel, Noel,*
> *Born from the womb of our fertile earth.*

In ancient times, with the trees as our home
Amid the savannahs we first set to roam
In nature's trust we began to explore
Guided on by the Spirit to many a shore.
Noel, etc.
And this birthing forth mid danger and hope
Sustained by the earth as our periscope.
Our daily food from earthly resource
Sustained our spirits and kept us on course.
Noel, etc.
We grew up erect and explored the new land
and from Africa moved with an outreach that fanned
With our planet'ry gaze and God's spirit as guide
Our homeland became a world so wide.
Noel, etc.
We oft got it right and sometimes went wrong
but always evolved mid the earth's fertile song.
While now so advanced, again we connect
With our African home, to regain our respect.

So, when you next celebrate Christmas, how will you give birth to new life? It may be attending lovingly to the hurt and pain of a loved one within or beyond your own family. It may be some new way to accommodate the other beings who share Planet Earth with us, particularly those among the threatened species. It may be a call to eco-justice, tending the earth and its resources with a great sense of responsibility, dignity and moral awareness.

So, why not call forth the creative artist within you and write a poem, sketch a drawing or sculpt an image to personalize for yourself this power of birthing so central to our Christmas celebration?

Chapter Four

Rebirthing the Inner Child — beyond unprocessed childhood fears

When one is at home in oneself, one is integrated and enjoys a sense of balance and poise. In a sense that is exactly what spirituality is: the art of homecoming. John O'Donohue.

Several years ago, two American scholars, Roger Moore, a psychiatrist, and Douglas Gillette, a mythologist, co-authored as series books on four male archetypes: the king, warrior, magician, and lover. Frequently they reference the inner child as a central dynamic in the growth and development of every person. (Moore & Gillette 1990). The notion of the inner child was first highlighted by the psychologist Carl G. Jung and may be described as a part of our subconscious development that has been picking up messages long before we were able to fully process what was going on (mentally and emotionally). The inner child can hold emotions, memories, and beliefs from the past as well as hopes and dreams for the future.

Moore and Gillette make the astute observation that if the inner child has been neglected or suppressed in our early formative years, it can manifest in later life in a compulsive desire for domination and control. They go on to suggest that several men with an intense need for such control are actually scared of their inner child (which they have never integrated), and therefore they require everybody around them to behave like children rather than as mutual adults. In other words, such men cannot tolerate other adults being adult and will try to control them as passive children. At a deeper psychological level, such men are projecting their wounded child onto others, because they have failed to do the inner work of integrating the inner child.

Many world leaders, mostly male, adopt dictatorial approaches and are threatened by any challenges to their imperial-type leadership. It is likely that they have not come to terms with their wounded child. Also, they may well have risen to the top because they are driven to prove their worth over and over. Unfortunately they then go on to wound a lot of others, culminating a world where our social policies, our politics and our economics are dysfunctionally destructive. And all the world religions, at one time or another, show evidence of this same woundedness.[3]

Popular Christmas devotions around the world focus strongly on the child in the crib. In devotional terms the focus on the baby child, vulnerable and at risk, evokes emotional sentiments of love and care, a response that is admirable and to be commended. Subconsciously, however, is the subtle message that childlikeness, which sometime gets confused with childishness, is a special predisposition through which we can best obtain favours from God. All too easily this can lead to co-dependence and passivity, with a tendency to blame ourselves as sinful and unworthy, thus needing the child-God to rescue us and make us right again.

Consequently, we now need to ask: How might the birthing archetype liberate and empower us to move beyond the childlike co-dependency and embrace the adult maturity suggested by the integration of the inner child? How can we re-envisage the child-God to represent the adult, internalising a more adult sense of faith and coming of age with the maturity desired in the words "I call you friends not servants." (Jn.15:15). More precisely, can we view the infant in the crib as a symbol of the inner child, calling us all to a deeper integration – psychologically and spiritually? And how might

---

[3] Some analysts will describe this as a process of internalized oppression. For more see webpage: https://en.wikipedia.org › wiki › Internalized_oppression

the Christmas carols that focus on the child open us up to such empowering possibilities?

1. Birthing the Inner Child (When a child is born)

The best known version of the song is probably the Jack Gold produced version for the singer Johnny Mathis, topping the British charts for three weeks in December, 1976. It was originally written by an Italian composer Ciro Dammicco in 1974. Later translated into English by the Austrian lyricist, Fred Jay, it became a popular Christmas Carol.

The adaptation below is an attempt to reclaim the inner child as a basis on which we can all grow into that fullness of life wherein we can work more zealously to build up on earth the empowering vision of the New Reign of God.

> *A ray of hope glistens all around*
> *the stars of heaven explode with sound*
> *and the stardust flows mid creative strain*
> *earth's seedling sprouts for all is germane*
> *Every human life sails the seven seas*
> *And the winds of life whisper in the trees*
> *And the parents love mid erotic hue.*
> *envelops life when the child is true.*
> *The eyes will gaze as we contemplate*

The inner child to negotiate

The trust and love for life to sustain

to keep the adult on a fertile plain.

(Spoken Text) We embrace the inner child, our basic love and security and the freedom of spirit whereby every person is accepted for who they are. and with all earth's creatures we journey forth, commissioned as all are to bring about a new heaven and new earth where love and justice can reign supreme.

A noble dream to which all aspire

to warm hearts with the Spirit's fire

Every child will laugh and the adult too

May our Christmas hope be a dream come true.

2. We pray for Protection (Away In A Manger)

It is generally considered that this carol was written in the mid-1800s by an anonymous American. The tune was composed by a J. E. Clark and later developed by Charles Hutchinson Gabriel of Grace Methodist Episcopal Church in the USA.

Several early publications ascribe the words to Martin Luther, some going so far as to title the carol "Luther's Cradle Song" or "Luther's Cradle Hymn". An American historian, Richard Hill, suggested in 1945 that *Away in a Manger* might have originated in a play for children to act, or a story about Luther celebrating Christmas with his own children, likely connected with the 400th anniversary of the reformer's birth in 1883.

While honouring the obvious appeal for children, we can reword this carol to embrace and include sentiments of joy arising from creation at large, desiring a more just and peaceful world for children and adults alike.

Midst echoes of warfare, a world in dread,
A new born baby, lays down his dear head.
A mother has laboured a birthing new life,
A father keeps vigil, protection from strife.
The stars in the night sky keep vigil replete,
The midwife is busy, her duty complete.
And siblings excited to see the new life,
And longing so deeply for peace beyond strife.
The cattle are lowing, the baby awakes,
Adjusting the senses, mid nature's own stakes.
The world is safe to the mind of a child,
Too quickly 'twill change, as life is beguiled.

The prayer of a mother, protection she seeks
from the God who is closer than words can decree.
Please stay with this baby till morning is nigh,
And the dawning of hope will be our supply.

The Little Drummer Boy

"**The Little Drummer Boy**" (originally known as "**Carol of the Drum**") is a popular Christmas song written by American composer Katherine Kennicott Davis in 1941. First recorded in 1951 by the Trapp Family, the song was further popularized by a 1958 recording by the Harry Simeone Chorale; the Simeone version was re-released successfully for several years, and the song has been recorded many times since then. In the lyrics, the singer relates how, as a poor young boy, he was summoned by the Magi to the Nativity of Jesus. Without a gift for the Infant, the little drummer boy played his drum with approval from Jesus's mother, Mary, recalling, "I played my best for him" and "He smiled at me".

Today the drum is a favourite instrument in men's rights of passage, as males consciously seek to reclaim a more authentic way of being an adult man in meaningful and empowering engagement with all other humans and with the planet entrusted to human care.

Come, and join with us, we're drumming for peace.
Come share our melody, in drumming release.
And open up your hearts with drumming increase,
Our adult faith proclaim, our drumming wont cease,
in peace - we release. .
So we've come of age, pa rum pum pum pum
Each one a wisdom sage, pa rum pum pum pum.

To build a world renewed, pa rum pum pum pum,

embracing old and youth, pa rum pum pum pum Rum pum pum pum, rum pum pum pum.

Mother Mary hummed, pa rum pum pum pum

The ox and lamb kept time, pa rum pum pum pum.

Creation's pulsing heart, pa rum pum pum

Every creature joins the melody, pa rum pum pum pum

And creation smiles in graceful joy,

To welcome all who share the earth's decoy,

We play the drum aloud for world peace,

Cir - cling for dialogue to release.

parum pum pum pum, Rum pum pum pum, rum pum pum pum.

Let every nation play the drum of peace — pa rum pum pum pum — pum pum, pum,

Chapter Five

Birthing in the Power of Womanhood

Regarding Mary, Catholics developed a severe case of fixation, while Protestants developed a severe case of amnesia... Stubbornly unwilling to abandon this woman to her imprisonment behind patriarchal bars, women are risking new, liberating interpretations of her meaning. Elizabeth Johnson.

Of all the human characters associated with the Christmas story, none is more outstanding than the woman named as Mary, mother of Jesus. Frequently named as virgin and mother, her status and meaning as a woman has been largely overshadowed and used across the Christian centuries to the detriment and degradation of women at large.

How to rebirth Mary herself is foundational to any reconstruction of Christmas and its meaning for the 21st century. With the rise of feminism in the 19th century, and the long struggle even to obtain basic voting rights, the widespread marginalization and oppression of women came to the fore. It continues to be a major cultural challenge in several parts of the contemporary world. And religion continues to be a substantial barrier to that fuller integration of women and their giftedness to human society.

The inherited Christian story of Mary usually translates into a dangerously misleading and oppressive narrative. In Christian art, Mary tends to be depicted as a young Caucasian, devotionally subdued, obedient, and subservient. Catholics claim that she was herself immaculately conceived at birth and elevated straight from earth to heaven at her death. Her body seems to be an obstacle that has to be rendered redundant as far as possible, in case there might be any residue of human sin or frailty that would make her unsuitable as a carrier of divine life.

Her pregnancy and the birth of Jesus are shrouded in mystery, allegedly impregnated not by any human male but by some unique intervention of the Holy Spirit of God. Nothing strange about this claim; in fact, it makes a great deal of sense, since the Spirit is the primary energizer of all creative endeavours including human fertilization, the difference being that human agency is largely subverted in the case of Mary.

Dualistic Splitting

Mary is declared to be a *virgin*, which in biological terms means that her hymen has not been penetrated and therefore she has never had sexual intercourse with a man. The first obstacle we encounter here is that of dualistic splitting. The sacred and the secular must be kept well apart. Accordingly, anything to do with divinity must be exclusively spiritual and as distinctly clear as possible from anything to do with human or earthly reality. Although God has created the world, God in himself is totally separated from such a creation, and all the more so, since the creation is deemed to be corruptible and transitory.

Such binary opposition belongs primarily to classical Greek philosophy. The following are just a few of the juxtaposed opposites: earth v. heaven, body v. soul, matter v. spirit. When it comes to Mary the mother of Jesus, the dualistic split is that of the human v. the divine, with Mary declared to be immaculately conceived, totally free from error or sin. All that belongs to the divine realm is pure and holy and must never be contaminated by the sinfulness of the human condition.

Consequently, for God to enter our world through the human requires an exceptionally holy person, uncontaminated by the affairs of daily life. Moreover, the entry and birth of such a person must be as miraculous as possible, highlighting the exalted status of the divine above and beyond the human. Similar characteristics are also attributed to other outstanding heroes of divine significance, (e.g., the Graeco-Roman Mithras, the Egyptian Horus, the Iranian Zoroaster, the Greek Helios).

Addressing the sexual undercurrents is a much more formidable task. In the case of Mary's pregnancy, sexual intercourse is totally subverted and portrayed as some kind of evil force from which a divine or holy person must be completely separated. There is no recognition of the fact that God is also the creator of human sexuality along with the central role of the erotic and sensuous pleasure in the mediation and expression of love. To the contrary, sex is portrayed as a supreme evil to be avoided at all costs. Such demonisation of human sexuality is at the root of much of the sexual repression and abuse so rampant in our world today.

Finally, we need to clear away the racism and ethnic undercurrents too long taken for granted. Across the Christian world, even to this day, Mary is depicted in art and sculpture as a white Western European woman, frequently portrayed with hands joined and head bowed in obedient submission. The original Palestinian woman of dark skin and robust personality is suppressed amid a cult of European colonialism.

How did Mary become pregnant?

What we have in the infancy narratives — in the Gospels of Matthew and Luke — is an idealization, heavily contaminated with what Elizabeth Johnson (2003, 28) describes as "an increasingly strong torrent of misogyny against women and their bodies." In the over-spiritualized account, Mary is impregnated by the Holy Spirit of God. Accordingly, we are offered an explanation based around Mary's virginity, suggesting that she was not impregnated in the usual human process of sexual intercourse. Describing Mary's virginity, we encounter a confusing picture between the Greek *parthenos* and the Hebrew *almah* (cf. Is.7:14). Had Isaiah wished to speak about a virgin (in the biological sense), he would have used the word *betula*, not *almah*. The word *betula* appears frequently in the Jewish Scriptures and is the only word, in both biblical and modern Hebrew, that conveys the need for sexual purity.[4]

In the Hebrew Scriptures, *almah* denotes a young woman of marriageable age and of outstanding character. Theologian Elizabeth Johnson (2003, p 239) affirms a more ancient and archetypal meaning for virginity: "To be a virgin is to be one in yourself, free, independent, insubordinated, unexploited, a woman never subdued."

---

[4] In fact, although Isaiah used the Hebrew word *almah* only once (7:14), the prophet uses this word *virgin* (betulah) five times throughout the book of Isaiah (23:4; 23:12; 37:22; 47:1; 62:5). Noteworthy, too is the derivation of *almah* from the Persian Al-Mah, the unmated moon goddess. Another cognate of this term was the Latin *alma*, "living soul of the world," which is essentially identical to the Greek *psyche*, and the Sanskrit *shakti*.

Here's a lightly expanded version of the text, keeping changes minimal but adding a few sentences to make it longer:

As already noted, the infancy narratives seem to have borrowed from the birth stories of other outstanding holy people. These parallels reflect a recurring tendency in religious traditions to frame significant figures within archetypal story patterns that resonate across cultures. While such narratives have no historical foundation (in all probability), we must not dismiss them as mere legend. Instead, these stories reveal archetypal truths interwoven into the fabric of human experience, pointing us to a "surplus of meaning" deserving a more nuanced and discerning pursuit of truth. By delving deeper into these truths, we uncover layers of symbolic and spiritual significance that extend beyond historical concerns.

Intriguingly, it is precisely when we recapture the uniqueness of Mary as a historical cultural personage — as Elizabeth Johnson (2003) does with remarkable ingenuity — that her archetypal significance is truly illuminated. Mary stands as a pivotal figure where history and archetype converge, embodying the sacred feminine in ways that transcend her immediate cultural context. In and through Mary, the womb of God and the womb of the universe are one, and birthing is the enduring legacy within which every creature — and not merely humans — is missioned for the work of co-creation. Her role reminds us of the deep interconnection between divine creativity and the ongoing unfolding of life across all dimensions of existence.

The Virgin archetype has an intense inner focus. She is spiritually oriented and more concerned with the inner world than the outer realm. Yet, from deep within that inner depth is a resourcefulness capable of birthing forth life at every level of creation, from the vast galaxies to minuscule subatomic particles. For women particularly, the archetype represents a sexualized fertility not to be confined to intimate partnerships, motherhood, or child rearing.[5]

Untold damage has been done by the literalization of Mary's virginity in the infancy narratives. In devotional terms, Mary is often described as the one who totally submits to God's will, allowing all that is unique to her femininity and capacity for mothering to be sacrificially undermined. Thus Mary is often portrayed as a model of loyal obedience, passively allowing God to do with her whatever God wants. All sense of adult engagement is suppressed for both God and Mary.

Such "loyal obedience" has been invoked down through the

---

[5] Not surprising, therefore, we find the paradoxical reality among the ancient Goddesses that they are often unmarried, but this did not mean that they were necessarily asexual. In fact, some of the virgin goddesses expressed their sexuality openly, owning their sexuality proudly and without shame. It was not given away or bartered or owned by their partners, but was wholly and solely within their own dominion.

centuries to relegate women to passive roles and foment greater allegiance to the institutional church. We need a more empowering Mariology, which in turn will be empowering for women (and men) as well as for the fertile creation itself which we humans, and all other beings, inhabit. It is that enlarged archetypal vision we need to recapture in the Christmas carols specifically devoted to Mary.

1. The Virgin-Woman's Birthing (Mary's Boy Child)

Sometime in the early 1950s, the black songwriter and choral conductor Jester Hairston was asked to provide a new Christmas carol for a concert by Walter Schumann's Hollywood Choir. Hairston thought back to a song he had composed a few years earlier for a West-Indian party, in which he used a calypso rhythm. He penned some new Christmas-themed lyrics for the melody and came up with this popular Christmas song.

Later, the American singer-cum-activist, Harry Belafonte, heard Schumann's choir sing this song and asked permission to record it for his 1956 album *An Evening with Belafonte*. The following year, "Mary's Boy Child" was a number one hit single for Belafonte. Other performers have also enjoyed success with this same hymn, and it has found its way into numerous hymnals around the world.

In this new version, I seek to highlight the archetypal

meaning of virginity as the capacity for birthing universal life, a creativity born of the energizing power of the God named in several indigenous cultures as the Great Spirit.

Mary's dream for all our race was born on Christmas Day
The virgin-woman impregnates mid creation's grand display.
Long time repressed mid forced control, with scripture Misconstrued
Virgin-woman now gives birth with grace and fortitude.
Hark, we now this great breakthrough, this new birth liberates.
So all can live in radiant hope, and celebrate today
While refugees amid their plight, traverse by land and sea
They sense a welcome and new home and a promise once more free.
Hark, we now this great breakthrough, this new birth liberates.
So all can live in radiant hope, and celebrate today
For a moment the world was aglow, all the bells rang out
There were tears of joy and laughter, people shouted
"Let everyone know, there is hope for all to find peace"

> *O Great Spirit, Your light will guide us*
> *O Great Spirit, Journey beside us*
> *O Great Spirit, Never forsake us.*
> *May true love reign once more!*
> *O Great Spirit, In Mary's rebirthing*
> *O Great Spirit, Love every earthling*
> *O Great Spirit, every heart stirring*

Celebrate life evermore!

O Great Spirit, Peace to our world

O Great Spirit, Justice unfurled

O Great Spirit, Hope is our herald

And every voice will sing

In joy and gratitude!

2. Mary Did you know your power for Transformation? (Mary did you know?)

This is a Christmas song addressing Mary, mother of Jesus, with lyrics written by Mark Lowry in 1984 and music written by Buddy Greene in 1991. It was originally recorded by Christian recording artist Michael English on his self-titled debut solo album in 1991. The song has since gone on to become a modern Christmas classic, recorded by hundreds of artists over the years, across multiple genres. Several recordings have reached the top ten in the *Billboard* R&B and Holiday charts. The song encourages contemplation of the relationship between Mary and Jesus, her son.

This hymn needs to be rewritten, acclaiming Mary as an outstanding Palestinian woman, deeply immersed in her earthly feminine wisdom and correspondingly bearing archetypal significance for all women (and indeed for men as well). For a fuller elaboration of these aspirations see the deeply inspiring read from the American theologian, Elizabeth Johnson (2003).

Mary did you know the archetypal wisdom you carried in your soul
Mary did you know the power for birthing life that recreates the whole.
Did you know the ancient wisdom calling you apart
to birth afresh for all new freedom of the heart
Mary did you know the liberating feminine that every woman knows
Mary did you know the fertile seeds of life which every garden grows
Did you know joy of intercourse for new life to beget
And undo the long repression of patriarchal debt
Let truth come forth, let music reign, let every woman rise
Let earth exult, in fertile force, may every being rejoice.
Mary did you know the power for transformation you set free
Mary did you know, the price you paid for creation's liberty?
Mary of our birthing, befriend us lest we stray
May we be your loyal companions all the way.

3. In the Power of Birthing (The Virgin Mary had a Baby Boy)

The Virgin Mary Had a Baby Boy is thought to have been composed in the early 1950s by Jamaican singer-songwriter Oswald Dunbar. The song became popular in the Caribbean and was later adapted by American folk singer Pete Seeger. It has been covered by many artists over the years, including Harry Belafonte, Mahalia Jackson, and The Kingston Trio.

This hymn needs to be rewritten so as to honour the Mary's virginity, not understood in narrow biological terms, but in its deep archetypal significance, as a capacity for birthing all forms of new life, from the vast galaxies to the tiny specks of dust.

> *The virgin Woman mid her birthing joy (x 3)*
> *Gives birth to all creation!*
> *CHORUS: The Heavens sing her glory*
> *In the radiant Spirit of life*
> *And everyone's creating,*
> *in the wisdom of midwife.*
> *Our faith is changed forever, yes, indeed, forever.*
> *The Heavens sing her glory*
> *In the radiant Spirit of life.*
> *The Heavens exult in all she creates (x 3)*
> *And it radiates her beauty.*
> *And for every mother who births new life (x 3)*
> *evolution sings with glory.*
> *Our Christmas song full of Mary's hope (x 3)*
> *empowers a new beginning.*

4. Mary Gentle, yet so Strong (Gentle Mary Laid her child)

This hymn was written in 1917 by English-born, Canadian educated Methodist minister Joseph Simpson Cook (1859-1933). Cook entered a Christmas carol-writing contest in 1919 in which this hymn won him first prize. Since many of the Protestant carols seemed to neglect Mary, Cook sought to elevate Mary's significance in the Christmas celebration. The adopted tune is from the Spring Carol **"Tempus Adest Floridum"** of the 16th century, using a melody more commonly associated with the carol, **"Good King Wenceslas."**

It was first published in the Christian Guardian in 1919 under the title 'The Manger Carol' and was used extensively by United Church of Canada congregations.

Once again, this hymn needs to be rewritten in line with the emerging insights of contemporary feminist thought and its relationship to Christian theology, honouring the enlarged scope for archetypal birthing already referenced above.

*Gentle Mary laid her hope in empowering freedom
As a woman of our race from oppression heal them.
Chosen one you lead the way - birthing new horizon
Recreating the world anew, refresh the sacred therein.
Mary gentle, yet so strong, birthing in creation
Calling forth empowering grace freedom's own gestation
Co-creating with the new, gift of evolution,
Vast the creaturely array, gifted contribution.
Gentle Mary prototype, every man and woman
Honouring the feminine faithfully in turn.
We include creation too, ever new a birthing,*

Every woman, man and child, every sacred earthling.

Woman gentle, yet so strong, birthing right relating
All who hunger for new life, in the Spirit's weighting.

Eco-justice calls us forth, to build the world anew
And birth once more for every being fulfilment to pursue.

Part Two

Carols in a New Language

for the 21st century

In part two of this book, I continue to rework a number of well known Carols, adopting the language to suit the underlying themes that emerge when we look more deeply at the meaning of Christmas.

I want to rescue the Carols from the traditional devotionalism, focussed on an all-powerful God coming to rescue powerless sinners. In that process, I want to reclaim the empowerment proclaimed by Jesus in the Gospel strategy known as the Kingdom of God. In this new liberating vision, I want to honour the enlarged horizons adopted by Jesus. These include not merely all peoples of other faiths and cultures but the entire web of life, from the vast galaxies down to the subatomic particles. All are revelations of God's creativity and subliminally all sing to the glory of God.

Such an understanding of God becomes much more transparent when we move away from the notion of a ruling God and instead reclaim a Christmas metaphor of enormous significance, namely *birthing*. As indicated in Part One, Mary the Virgin belongs to an ancient tradition in which virginity denotes a readiness for birthing new life across the entire spectrum of God's creation. Tragically, this ancient wisdom has been desecrated by reducing Mary's story to biological virginity, which has been the source of so much oppressive misogyny in Christianity and in the other major religions as well.

These liberating and empowering themes are not unique to Christianity. Deep down, all religions adopt these aspirations, but, sadly, have also largely neglected them. This might well be the reason why many reflective people today move beyond religion and instead seek alternative ways to express their sense of mystery, holiness (wholesomeness), and a deeper connection with the spirit-power that animates and sustains the entire creation. For such people, the reflections of this small book may have much to offer.

Back in 1967, the British Benedictine monk, Sebastian Moore, wrote a book entitled *God is a New Language*, stating boldly that if Christianity is to survive, it must learn to communicate in terms intelligible to our times and relevant for the enlarged worldview that now engages us all. Although published almost sixty years ago, this book has an enduring relevance and sustains a still largely unanswered response. Hopefully, my attempt to rework the carols in language more suitable for our time will encourage other potential readers to embrace the same endeavour. It is a call to our creativity, our service to the new hope so many hunger for in the world today.

Chapter One

Carols for Everyone, Christian or Otherwise

God is endlessly emerging from the staggering complexity of all humanity's aspirations across time. Nancy Ellen Abrams.

The Christian celebration of Christmas is based on the opening Chapters of two Gospels, those of Matthew and Luke. For much of Christian history, that material was taken literally. God worked a miracle, through which Mary was able to conceive and give birth to Jesus without a biological father. And while his own Jewish people did not welcome Jesus ("He came to his own and they received him not — Jn. 1:11), angelic heavenly hosts hailed his arrival, as did shepherds and wise men.[6] Meanwhile, Joseph filled the gap to make

---

[6] The need to confront the antisemitism in the Christmas narrative is addressed by Peter Keenan (2021)

up for the missing biological father.

Those who consciously adopt the Christian faith still take much of the story at its face value and believe that God sent Jesus (his beloved Son) to bring salvation and redemption to this sin-laden world. A growing body of more reflective Christians, impacted by the critical consciousness of our time, are slow to accept angelic interventions, virgin births, and the kind of mythic narrative upon which they perceive the Gospel story to be based.

Furthermore, let us acknowledge those many non-religious people who join the Christmas festivities, support carol services for various charities, make gifts, join the sense of joviality, and some even go to Church on Christmas day as a gesture of solidarity with family and loved ones. One wonders what the Christmas carols mean for these folks. Do they ever stop and ask what the words actually signify? Or is it a case of being carried along by the archetypal force of the melody as I briefly explain in Chapter One?

For religious people and non-religious alike, the Christmas Carols can carry meaning, possibly to quite some depth. And if the Carols spoke a language that could be heard by such people, then presumably that sense of meaning would be more readily engaging. In this case, I am not hoping that they might return and reclaim a religious faith. That is not my goal. I am not really worried whether or not they return to religion. It is deeper archetypal engagement and inspiration I am interested in, which I do believe is spiritual, but not necessarily religious.

Let's have a look at three Carols with a central theme that seems quite secular, yet conveys a lure to deeper meaning as we sing or hum along with the melody.

1. **May our Ships Sail Safely Home** (I saw three ships come sailing in)

The earliest printed version of this carol is from the 17th century, possibly Derbyshire (UK), and was also published by the English lawyer and antiquarian, William Sandys, in 1833.

The lyrics mention the ships sailing into Bethlehem, but the nearest body of water is the Dead Sea about 20 miles (32 km) away. The reference to three ships is thought to originate in the three ships that bore the purported relics of the Biblical magi (three wise men) to Cologne Cathedral in the 12th century. Another possible reference is to Wenceslaus II, King of Bohemia, who bore a coat of arms "Azure three galleys argent". And a third suggestion is that the ships actually refer to the camels used by the Magi, when camels were frequently referred to as "ships of the desert".

In the opening decades of the 21st century, the European world witnessed the death of many asylum seekers crossing the Mediterranean Sea and other troubled waters in search of a better life. Many of them never made it, despite having paid much money to smugglers whose "ships" were often unsuited for such perilous journeys. Let us remember these victims carrying the pain and anguish of so much poverty and tragedy in our world, and let's hope that the ships that sail our seas can offer greater protection, reassurance, hope, and freedom for future migrants.

> *I saw three ships come sailing in*
> *Mid Christmas fray, and everyday;*
> *Mid troubled waves to calm the sea*
> *And reach safe port in the morning.*
> *The ships had made it through the night,*
> *Mid Christmas fray, and everyday?*
> *Proclaiming peace to all on earth,*
> *And reach safe port in the morning.*
> *And all the bells rang out with joy,*
> *Mid Christmas fray, and everyday.*
> *An end to war, let peace prevail,*
> *And reach safe port in the morning.*
> *And every port across the globe*
> *Mid Christmas fray, and everyday;*
> *There's safe asylum here for all,*
> *With harbour space in the morning.*
> *Let no one out on troubled seas*
> *Mid Christmas fray and everyday.*

Let all be safe in love and care
With harbour space in the morning.

2. Joy in Defiance (Joy to the World)

"Joy to the World" is an English Christmas carol, written in 1719 by the English minister and hymn writer Isaac Watts, and its lyrics are an interpretation of Psalm 98 adopted to celebrate the birth of Jesus Christ. Today, the carol is usually sung to an 1848 arrangement by the American composer, Lowell Mason.

We sing this song in a kind of prophetic defiance. For millions in our world deprived of basic resources and afflicted by war, exploitation, and poverty, and more recently by treacherous weather conditions, joy does not come easily. Yet, the human spirit hungers for that wholeness which it deems to be a basic right for every living being, human and non-human alike.

Joy to the world! Let sorrows cease!
Let peace come forth for all.
Let every heart now breaking
And every limb now aching,
Break free from all oppression
Bring healing to aggression,
And set, then set, all creatures free.
Joy to the world! Keep hope alive;

Let justice shine for all;
May all who work transforming
To comfort all the mourning
With peace amid all conflict
And reconcile the convict,
 And set, then set, all creatures free. .
Joy to the world, we care for Earth
Let living soil produce.
The pain of land exploited
Mid floods and fires ignited.
Give all clean drinking water
And food for those who falter
And set, then set, all creatures free.
Joy to the world, there's hope for all
Let all oppression cease.
As we create new bridges
 To end dividing ridges.
And bring together all nations
Encircling celebrations
And set, then set, all creatures free.

3. Blessed be Our Trees! (O Christmas Tree)

O Tannenbaum, a traditional German folk song, became associated with the traditional Christmas tree. The modern lyrics were written in 1824 by the Leipzig organist, teacher, and composer, Ernst Anschütz. *Tannenbaum* is a fir tree. The lyrics do not actually refer to Christmas, or describe a decorated Christmas tree. Instead, they refer to the fir's evergreen quality as a symbol of constancy and faithfulness. The custom of the Christmas tree developed in the course of the 19th century, and the song came to be seen as a Christmas Carol.

The tree is a religious symbol of great age and known across all religious traditions. It is also a symbol of the Great Earth Mother Goddess, going back into deep time. Several legends are known across the world on the healing properties of trees and the central importance of trees in terms of ecological equilibrium.

The stripping away of forests, whether to access mineral resources in the Southern Philippines, or to create more land to feed cattle (and produce meat) in the Brazilian Amazon, leave a range a devastating consequences for people and local environments.

The Christmas tree, therefore, can be viewed not merely as a decoration in our homes but as an enduring symbol of earth's vitality, a natural resource that needs to be protected and preserved in a much more ethically informed way.

> *O Christmas tree, O Christmas tree!*
> *Your ageless symbol tall and free.*
> *In every faith known to our race*

You hold a special, sacred place.
O tree of life and fruitful gift
We are your guests this Christmas time.
O Christmas tree, O Christmas tree,
From Spring-like sprig to Summer fruit
From Autumn down till Winter's rest
You represent life's cyclic crest.
Adorning life on our pathway
And share our space this Christmas time.

O Christmas tree, O Christmas tree,
How sturdy stands your dignity
Amid the storms and the rains
And ever fed by sunlight's gains.
Mid scorching sun or glistening snow
All held in place this Christmas time.

O Christmas tree, O Christmas tree,
So oft chopped down in thoughtless spree.
Mid mountains bare and valley doom
where mudslides cause such painful gloom.
Forgive the wrong we oft accrue
As we befriend your Christmas hue.

Chapter Two

It is time to Outgrow the Imperial Language

The stories of the first Christmas are pervasively anti-imperial... God's dream for us is not simply peace of mind, but peace on earth. Marcus Borg & John D. Crossan

The rebirthing we celebrate at Christmas is best understood against the vast backdrop of all that has been birthed in the cosmic creation of 13.8 billion years, in earth's own evolution beginning some four billion years ago, and in our God-given human story of seven million years of formative growth and development.

In more recent millennia, we began to take a different direction as we settled in fixed places and became a much more sedentary species. It reaped great benefits but also some deeply disturbing deviations, none more problematic than the arrogant patriarchal power we began to exercise over the land and subsequently over all other life-forms. Central to this notion of imperial power was the evolution of kings, kingdoms, and strategies of patriarchal control and domination.

In a masterly piece of scholarly research, the British historian, Dominic Lieven, in his book *In the Shadow of the Gods* (Lieven 2022), traces the long history of kingship on a global scale. It is widely assumed that kingship is a very ancient institution, one that has been around for several thousands of years. Not so, according to Lieven, who claims that it is little more than 6,000 years old, first rising in the ancient Akkadian empire (approx. modern day Iraq and Iran) around 2,500 BCE, and subsequently spreading throughout the wider world well into the 1800s CE.

Lieven also traces a common originating source for all forms of ancient kingship, namely worship of a ruling sky God, whose wisdom is to guide the king and whose power from on high validates all his earthly efforts at domination and control.[7] In the Judaeo-

---

[7] Here the reader needs to keep in mind that the notion of the ruling Sky-God was itself created by human projection, as power-hungry humans sought validation for their desire to dominate and control. In ancient times, God was envisaged more as a Spirit-based life-force, at work throughout the entire creation, an understanding of God still espoused by indigenous, tribal/first-nations people across the modern world (more in O'Murchu 2011).

Christian tradition we note this understanding of kingship throughout the Old Testament (the Hebrew Scriptures), with Jesus postulated to be authentically divine because it is claimed that he is descended directly from the great King David.[8] And for much of the Christian story, the power attributed to holy rulers (Popes, Bishops, and even clergy) is constructed around this ancient notion of divine imperialism.[9]

From about the middle of the 20th century, Scripture scholars and theologians began to raise serious doubts about the authenticity of such royal imperial claims. One American scholar Wes Howard Brook, offers this challenging statement: "Jesus of Nazareth proclaimed the 'reign of God' in accordance with the pattern of the religion of creation, while denouncing the religion of empire as a demonic counterfeit." (Howard-Brook 2016, xiii). On closer examination of the Gospel notion of the Kingdom of God, they began to realise that Jesus embraced a very different worldview, not an endorsement of kingship, but a substantial undermining of it

---

[8] Amazingly, the British historian, Dominic Lieven (2022), referenced above, never once refers to king Saul, with only a single reference to kings David and Solomon (ibid, 184), since most of what is said about them in Scripture is legendary and mythological and thus difficult to verify with any degree of historical accuracy.

[9] In an intriguing article in the British religious publication, *The Tablet* (December 2023), Bennett Zon, professor of music ad Durham University (UK), claims that some of the original versions of the Carol, Adeste Fidelis (O Come All Ye Faithful), was sung as a tribute to the English monarchy.

to the point of rejecting it completely. It was the Roman emperor, Constantine, and not Jesus or Paul, who laid the imperial foundations for the Christian faith.

The more authentic version of the historical Jesus is captured in these words from the Scripture scholar, John Dominic Crossan:

> God's kingdom was to be the final fulfilment of biblical dreams for a world of distributive justice, the ideal realization of biblical hopes for a world of cosmic nonviolence, and the climax of biblical promises for a world of universal peace… The specific phrase "Kingdom of God" is practically non-existent prior to Jesus' usage. So, a good translation should offer some hint as to why Jesus invented it as his own favourite designation for a transformed world and a transfigured earth. (Crossan, 2022, 282)

Note how Crossan highlights the cosmic and planetary dimensions. It seems that Jesus never envisaged this "New Reign of God" to be for humans only; it embraces the entire creation, human, earthly, and cosmic alike. Crossan also refers to the need to translate the imperial language into something that will explain in a more transparent way the bigger and deeper vision of Jesus. Following a suggestion made by Crossan himself many years ago, I adopt the phrase: *The Companionship of Empowerment*. Among other things, this translation is probably closer to the original Aramaic in which Jesus would have spoken. (More in O'Murchu 2019).

All the carols that reference or address God (or Jesus) as a king need to be rewritten. From a Christian point of view, this revision is necessary to bring the spirituality and theology up to date in terms of the leading scholarship of our time, in both scripture and theology. Second, the revision is also necessary for cultural reasons, as our world is growing weary of so many imperial power-games to the detriment of people and our responsibilities towards the earthly creation. Let's make our Christmas a time to call forth prophetic denunciation of false power, but also an opportunity to re-imagine what an empowering world order would begin to feel like.

1. Oh Universal Power of Three (We Three Kings of Orient are)

This Christmas carol was written by John Henry Hopkins Jr. in 1857. At the time, Hopkins served as the rector of Christ Episcopal Church in Williamsport, Pennsylvania (USA), and he wrote the carol for a Christmas pageant in New York City. It was the first widely popular Christmas carol written in America.

One way to reimagine this carol is by focussing on the figure of three, considered to be an ancient sacred number in all the major religions and, according to the cosmologist George Greenstein

(1988), a common configuration among galaxies and planets. Three also represents a communal construct, echoing archetypal vibrations for collaboration, togetherness, harmony, community building. Like several archetypes briefly reviewed in this book, the figure of three takes us beyond the individual person into the realm of the transpersonal, and beyond that into what physicists like Brian Swimme (2022) call the process of cosmogenesis.

All creation bears the trace
Number three in every place,
Stars galactic, planets vatic,
Ripples of harmony
CHORUS: Oh, Universal power of three
All connected flowing and free.
Held encircled, bright and sparkled
Music of the spheres.
All religion bears the trace.
Trinity in love embrace
All entangled, like triangle
As nothing stands alone.
Quarks and leptons too reveal
In that threesome sacred seal.
Spin and colour, cosmic fervour,
Beyond what we can see.

No more kings, imperial thrones
No more patriarchal clones.
Round the table, we are able
To recreate new hope.

2. Farewell to David's City (Once in Royal David's City)

Originally written as a poem by Irishwoman, Cecil Frances Alexander, this carol was first published in 1848 in her hymn book *Hymns for Little Children*. A year later, the English organist, Henry John Gauntlett, discovered the poem and set it to music.

In the spirit of the Romantic poetic era, Alexander follows close on what I describe elsewhere in this book as the devotion of consolation. Her description of Jesus as "little, weak, and helpless" invites us to being in solidarity with all who suffer, relying on our faith in Jesus to see us through life's struggles.

Moving from the devotion of consolation to the spirituality of liberation, this Carol can be heard afresh as a critique of the prevailing culture of imperialism, moving from the kingly foundation of David to the empowering vision of the liberating companionship, described in the Gospels as the Kingdom of God.

There's no king in David's city, there's no throne of kingly power.
All the talk of Empire building falters like a withered flower.
Toppling all the empire's glory in the breakthrough of this hour

Born to us a child prophetic, ushers in another way. Peace on earth, empowering justice, the disempowered will lead the way. In the circle of companions, empowering grace is here to stay.

David's city is collapsing like an empire's feet of clay. God's new reign is taking over weaving an empowering way. Now, we're called to work together co-creating God's new day.

Every empire lost its meaning in the name of Christmas day. Neither kings nor great messiahs Godlike goodness could display. Join together as companions weaving this non-violent way.

Bethlehem so small and lowly, David's trace cannot be seen. This is God without an Empire, violent power declared obscene. Peace on earth and transformation, a new horizon is foreseen.

Church is called to heed the message far from kings and kingly lore. Called to build a new communion and welcome all with open door. Immanuel is truly with us - rejoice we at this sacred hour.

3. **Good News of a Special Birth** (The Sussex Carol)

The Sussex Carol was first published by Luke Wadding, a 17th-century Irish bishop, in a work called *Small Garland of Pious and Godly Songs* (1684). It is unclear whether Wadding wrote the song or was recording an earlier composition. Both the text and the tune to which it is now sung were discovered and written down by Cecil Sharp in Buckland, Gloucestershire, and by Ralph Vaughan Williams, who heard it being sung by a Harriet Verrall of Monk's Gate, near Horsham, Sussex (hence "The Sussex Carol"). The tune to which it is generally sung today is the one Vaughan Williams took down from Mrs. Verrall and published in 1919.

Similar to many other carols, we encounter the language of God as a saving king whom we welcome and acclaim as the saviour of the world. Instead, we can hear the song as one of gratitude for God's goodness and the invitation to seek and protect that goodness in every aspect of creation.

> *On Christmas night all people's sing*
> *Acclaim good news with joy we bring*
> *A dispensation rare and new*
> *A sacred flame, a new breakthrough.*
> *CHORUS: This is good news of special birth,*
> *To set all free from morbid death.*
> *To lift up every struggling soul*
> *Empowering grace, the Spirit's breath.*
> *And nature joins the song's release*
> *All creatures seek justice in peace.*

Beyond the violence too long endured
A new prince leads with hope procured.
We move beyond what ages past
Declared to be our last resort.
God's Spirit lures another dawn
of birthing forth empowering love.

4. Blessed are the Poor in Spirit (Good King Winceslaus)

This carol tells the story of a Bohemian king who goes on a journey, braving harsh winter weather, to give alms to a poor peasant on the feast of Stephen (December 26). During the journey, his page is about to give up the struggle against the cold weather, but is enabled to continue by following the king's footprints, step for step, through the deep snow. The legend is based on the life of the historical Saint Wenceslaus I, Duke of Bohemia (907–935). In 1853, English hymn-writer, John Mason Neale, translated the lyric from a Czech poem by Václav Alois Svoboda, in collaboration with his music editor, Thomas Helmore.

The rewritten version below calls to mind the many people around our world unable to embrace the Christmas spirit of joy and celebration, due to poverty or oppression, and it goes on to echo a call to all people of good will to work for that justice that will lead to greater freedom and the ability to rejoice not merely at Christmas but throughout the entire year.

Many people give their lives to feed hungry needy Oft amid the snow and cold in conditions freezing. See the footsteps of the brave, reaching out to others. Little children cry for help held by loving mothers.

Why is earth divided up mid the rich and poor? Abundant life provides for all but many not secure. Let's get rid of greed and power with abundance flowing. Plenty for all upon the earth let love with justice grow.

Mid the glow of Christmas night some cry out in hunger. Others join in merriment, let us share the bumper. Birthing forth for every child promise for the future And for every adult too joy to truly nurture.

In our Godly steps we thread, where the snow lays dinted, Warming every human heart mid the frosty glinted. Therefore, loving ones be sure, wealth or rank possessing, Ye who now will bless the poor, shall yourselves find blessing.

Chapter Three

Decolonising the Christmas Carols

The Holy One comes to us in ordinary experience, which becomes extraordinary only through interpretation. James Carroll.
Jesus was born into a society traumatized by state violence. Karen Armstrong

Most of the best-known Christmas Carols were composed by Europeans, particularly in the 1800s, at a time when European colonialism prevailed across the world. Many also describe weather conditions — snow, frost, etc. — belonging to a Western European context. Today, with an estimated 80% of Christians living in the Southern hemisphere, devoid of the wintery conditions of the West, we need a more culturally-sensitive version of the Christmas Carols. Instead, we need to embrace the climatic emergency, which impacts upon all of us, and potentially with more deadly consequences for those living in the Southern hemisphere.

Several popular Christian hymns, including Christmas Carols, are couched in royal language, addressing or praising God and Jesus as a ruling king. This is the imperial legacy under review by several contemporary scripture scholars and theologians. This field of study is known as *postcolonialism,* largely a development of the mid-twentieth century and espoused in Christian studies throughout the closing decades of the 20th century (more in O'Murchu 2014). Postcolonialism is mainly concerned about the *residue* — the aftermath of the colonial mindset, which endures long after the colonial forces have left.

A classical contemporary example of the postcolonial residue is that of the oppressive strategy adopted by the one-time Zimbabwean president, Robert Mugabe (d. 2019), in his treatment of his own people. Mugabe contributed to the removal of the British colonizers from his native land. He helped to displace the external oppressor. Several years later, his regime within Zimbabwe sought to reclaim land from white farmers, brutalising thousands as the external oppressors (the British) had done to the black people 50-100 years previously. This was not merely an act of revenge, because it was activated in such a way that millions of black people also suffered significantly. Robert Mugabe had helped throw out the external oppressor (in 1980), but he had not expelled from his heart the residue of imperial terror and consequently, his internalised oppression took a toll on his own people — black and white — as severe as any brutality exerted by the external oppressor in former times.

It is much easier to expel the external oppressor than to undo the grip of internalized oppression. The former is overt and conscious, the latter is covert and deeply subconscious. A person, a group, or even a nation can convey a strong semblance of being externally free, while still harbouring within the crippling residue of a subjected people. Victims of physical, mental or sexual abuse can bury the effects deep inside for several years. It is consigned to a hidden woundedness that will never heal while it is buried so deeply. And it can be very scary to allow such dangerous stuff to come to the surface.

Change our Worldview

Finally, we need to note that several Christmas Carols adopt the notion of a three-tier universe, which science and cosmology has long outgrown. This is another residue we need to discard. The dualistic split between the all holy heaven above (from whence comes the saviour), and the sin-laden earth, sliced between Heaven and Hell, is a debilitating, paralysing construct devoid of hope and meaning in our time. Instead, the evolving cosmology of our age seeks to call forth humans as responsible Earthlings, to exercise their mission in a more inclusive and empowering way, for the benefit of the suffering earth itself and for all who are adversely affected by the exploitation of the earth's resources.

The imperial residue, identified by postcolonialism, undermines human agency and dignity on several levels including our relationship with land. No longer must we regard our Earth as merely a resource, indeed a commodity that exists for human well-being. In the Hebrew Scriptures, the land is God's great gift to the people, a resource to be used wisely and sustainably. Our ethical regard for the land and its resourcefulness has become ever more urgent and acute in the face of the several ecological emergencies of the 21st century.

Our contemporary theology of Incarnation embraces God's birthing in, and befriending of, all the embodied dimensions of creation, fromquarks to the farthest reaches of the universe. The Christmas Carols need to reflect and echo that same creative universality. Christmas can no longer serve merely as a reminder to humans of their need for salvation. It must also offer redemptive hope to all creatures who share creation with us. The inherited anthropocentric emphasis (as if only humans matter), must give way to the enlarged cosmic and planetary context. Above and beyond the yearnings of the human heart, we also need to hear the cries of the suffering earth and the divine embodiment reflected in all aspects of the cosmic creation.

Shifting the Focus

So many Carols, like several popular Christian hymns, are saturated with imperial language, lauding God — and Jesus — in honorific terms, as Lord and Ruler of the whole universe. Even the word *Lord*, used effusively in Christian prayer and liturgy, is borrowed from what Elizabeth Schussler Fiorenza (1992) describes as a social system known as *kyriarchy*, denoting domination, oppression, and submission. Even our use of the word *glory* in Christian prayer and liturgy is shrouded in imperial projections onto the one perceived to be superior to us and to all things on earth and therefore deserving of "glory, power, and praise." Inadvertently, and sometimes consciously, such a stance breeds an unhealthy sense of co-dependency, like a child responding to its parents in a childlike way, long after outgrowing childhood.

The following is an attempt on my part to render the Carols in language that transcends imperialism (all the references to kingship), subdues the patriarchal tone, and re-inscribes the inclusive, empowering dynamics more congruent with the vision of the Kingdom of God as the companionship of empowerment. I offer a sampled rewording of some of the better known carols, and in all cases I am retaining the standard music/melody.

1. Rid our World of Darkness (In the Bleak Mid winter)

Written initially by English poet, Christina Rossetti, it is commonly performed as a Christmas Carol. The poem was published under the title "A Christmas Carol" in the January 1872 issue of *Scribner's Monthly*, In 1906, the composer Gustav Holst composed a setting of Rossetti's words (titled "Cranham") in *The English Hymnal* which is sung throughout the world. An anthem setting by Harold Darke composed in 1909 is also widely performed by choirs.

In this rewording, the carol moves beyond the wintery weather conditions associated with Western countries and the Northern hemisphere. Instead we look at the bleakness of poverty, the darkness of oppression, and the wintery conditions of marginalisation that impact upon so many people (mainly in the Southern hemisphere). Let's hear the hymn as a cry for justice, liberation, generating new hope and meaning.

Mid the bleakness of our world, war and violence reign
Limiting our freedom, crucifying our pain.
Wounded people, hurting, earth in pain as well
Despite enduring bleakness, God will dwell!
Rid our world of darkness, let oppression cease
Let the earth so fertile recreate in peace.
No more wounded creatures anywhere on earth.

Touch the land with healing, bring new life to birth.

No more hungry children, no more wounded souls,

Open hearts receiving all the earth extolls.

The promised price of freedom everywhere on earth,

Get rid of all division, bring new life to birth

No more dislocation, driven far from home

seeking place of refuge after so much roam.

Welcome from all nations, no one left outside.

Be it crib or manger welcome here abide.

2. See amid the Season's Glow (See amid the Winter's snow)

This carol was, written by Edward Caswall and first published in 1858. In 1871 Sir John Goss composed a hymn tune for it.

Snow for people in colder latitudes can evoke awe and wonder as we behold the white carpet that transforms our landscape. It is however a largely Western reality, unknown to the millions of Christians (and others) in the South who will sing this Christmas hymn. In this rewording I expand the context from merely one season (Winter as understood in the West), to the various seasons that manifest ecological diversity and a range of possibilities for the earth's fertility to nurture not merely humans but many other creatures who share creation with us.

See, amid the season's glow
Fertile earth for all to sow.
Birthing forth for all to thrive
everything is now alive!

Chorus: Hail you creatures sing aloud
lift the veil of every shroud
Join the chorus to adorn
Welcome to this Christmas morn

See amid the season's glow
all creation seeks to grow
Every life a cherished place
every creature we embrace. Chorus.

See amid the season's glow
all the suff'ring must outgrow.
Peace and justice all around
And may good will for all abound.

See amid the season's glow
justice-makers rise to show
Another way the reconcile
with all condemned to their exile.

3. The Tree that Nourishes (The Holly and the Ivy)

"The Holly and the Ivy" is a traditional British folk Christmas carol, which can only be traced as far as the early nineteenth century, but the lyrics reflect an association between holly and Christmas, dating probably back to medieval times. The currently popular version was collected in 1909 by the English folk song collector, Cecil Sharp, in the market town of Chipping Campden in Gloucestershire, England, from a woman named Mary Clayton.

In this rewording, I once more celebrate the gift of trees with the tree as a universal religious symbol, and also as an icon of the interdependence with which everything in creation flourishes.

The holly and the ivy,
And all the forest trees
The beauty of our woodlands,
All that whisper in the breeze.

CHORUS: From the rising of the Sun
And the stars that shine so bright
Let every light illumine life
Set every wrong aright

In every ecosystem
Trees nurture and sustain
A vast array of nutrients
Enriching every plain.

The tree of life has flourished
In every sacred space
From ancient Goddess till our time
Bestows enduring grace.

The ancient vine of Israel
And Buddha-tree as well.
In every tree we see the face
of God among us dwell.

So, sing we glad and graceful
Enrich our Christmas joy,
For trees like sacred symbols,
Our truth will amplify.

For the poor and marginalized of our world, the Christmas Carols provide comfort and consolation, without necessarily contributing anything to the relief or reform of their plight. For the rich and powerful, the Carols can be a buffer preventing people from seeing, and attending to, the cry for justice and liberation arising from the millions of deprived people on our planet. For both groups, the focus on the vulnerable infant in the Christmas crib evokes childlike sentimentality and yearnings for the fulfilment of childhood hopes too long neglected. How might we revision the childlike devotion so as to move us in the direction of adult growth, maturity, and shared human responsibility in the name of justice and empowerment for all?

Chapter Four

Music of the Spheres: Even Creation Sings

Everything in the universe worked together to give birth to song, a song unutterable in the symbolic form of mathematics. Brian Swimme.

The Christmas season carries an aura of jubilation and celebration far beyond the so widely evident human merriment. It feels as if the whole creation is joining in the festivities. A similar feature is discernible as well in the Gospel narratives, particularly in the angelic voices coming from afar, acclaiming the newly born Christ-child.

Although derived from a Greek word, *angelos* (meaning messenger), the concept of angels seems to have started with Zoroastrianism, around the sixth century BCE and continues to be used extensively throughout the Judaeo-Christian Bible. In the Abrahamic religions, angels tend to be depicted as intermediaries between God (or Heaven) and humanity. They are often invoked as protectors and guides for humans, such as guardian angels and servants of God. In religious art, angels are usually shaped like humans of extraordinary beauty, while sometimes they are portrayed in a frightening, inhuman manner. They are often identified in Christian artwork with bird wings, halos, and divine light.

Their intermediary role reflects the three-tiered universe: heaven above, hell (Hades) below, and earth in between, probably borrowed from Zoroastrianism, a religion that also describes a cosmic clash between Ahura Mazda and Ahriman — forces of good and evil with their armies of angels and devils. Like Ahura Mazda, the Old Testament god, Yahweh, has an army of angels. These warrior angels battle against evil forces led by Satan, who resembles Ahriman.

The British journalist, Peter Stanford, explores the history of angels (Stanford 2022), past and present, highlighting their symbolic value as a meeting place for art, culture, and spirituality. Some years ago, a Canadian researcher, Carmen Boulter, offered an archetypal understanding of angels in her book, *Angels and Archetypes: An Evolutionary Map of Feminine Consciousness* (Boulter 1997). She explores the notion of archetypes through various Goddess traditions and their relevance for contemporary women in particular. I suggest that this fertile line of enquiry needs to be expanded beyond the human realm, since all archetypes are mediated for us humans in and through the wider web of the cosmic and planetary creation.

Fine Tuning Creation

Something of that same archetypal resonance has been pursued by some of the cutting edge science of the 20th and 21st centuries in the concept of *String Theory*. Beginning in the 1960s with notable scholars such as Yoichiro Nambu, Holger Bech Nielsen, and Leonard Susskind, the theory lost favour for much of the 1970s. It was subsequently revived by physicists John Schwarz and Michael Green, and it became a much more serious field of research in the 1990s under the American theoretical physicist Edward Witten. The theory claims that reality is made up of infinitesimal vibrating strings, smaller than atoms, electrons, or quarks. In other words, the fundamental energy of creation may be compared to the vibration of a guitar string, rather than a point-like structure such as an atom, or a subatomic particle.

It is suggested that creation moves and develops along wave-like energy-patterns (quantum theory), resonating harmoniously like musical echoes. To accommodate this visionary possibility, string theory goes on to suggest that our universe consists of *eleven* and not merely the four, dimensions of length, breadth, height, and time (the other seven being compacted in a manner not yet understood by science).

To most scientists string theory sounds strange and weird, similar to the concept of angels for many people of our time, religious and non-religious alike. Might it be as we enter and embrace the archetypal realm that we see both concepts as human attempts to name and engage with the mysterious nature of the world we inhabit? And surely, Christmas is a preeminent time to name and acclaim the rich possibilities of such esoteric ideas.

1. Silence of the Spheres (Silent Night)

As recently as 1995, an ancient manuscript of this hymn was discovered in Austria. The words were originally written in 1816 by a young Catholic priest, Fr. Joseph Mohr (d.1848), who employed a local school master and organist, Franz Xavier Gruber (d.1863), to compose the music in 1818, using a guitar, as the church organ had been damaged by flooding.

Life had been hard for the people in the little town of Mariapfarr, striving to recover from twelve years of war, further exacerbated by "The Year Without a Summer" (1816), in which crops failed, followed by widespread famine. Fr. Mohr's congregation was poverty-stricken, hungry, and traumatised. Against this anguished background, he crafted Holy Night, evoking the gift of God's peace for his troubled people.

Perhaps at no time in the song's history was this message more important than during the Christmas Truce of 1914, when, at the height of World War I, German and British soldiers on the front lines in Flanders laid down their weapons on Christmas Eve (Dec. 24th) and together sang "Silent Night".

In our time, let us also seek to recapture the paradox within and behind the silence we witness as we look out on the vast cosmic creation. Several lightyears away from us, far beyond the twinkling stars of a clear winter sky, is an enormous amount turbulence and sheer cacophony. In the words of the physicist, Michio Kaku, (1999, 172), "In the deep space, we must face the reality that most of the universe is in turmoil, with lethal radiation belts and swarms of deadly meteors." What kind of silence do we need to honour this paradox?

Silent night, Holy night; awesome echoes of starlight.
Cosmic birth pangs forever release, weaving patterns never cease.
Pulsating Spirit gives birth, now live forever on earth.

Silent night, Holy night; creation's grandeur, God's delight,
Ancient story come all this way, evolution is here to stay.
Spirit is silent and strong, weaving the new cosmic song.

Silent night, Holy night; humans called to gaze aright
A myst'ry great beyond our grasp, contemplate with earth at rest. Dawn
of every moon, Emmanuel come soon!

2. Led by the Light (Oh Holy Night)

The creation of this carol aptly represents something of the inclusive spirituality of the Christmas crib. It was composed by a Jewish man Adolphe Adam in 1843, based on a poem by a French atheist Placide Cappeau, rejected by the church in 1848 and eventually, in 1855, translated into English by an American Unitarian, John Sullivan Dwight.

In our time, the frequent references to stars and their gift of light open up a range of creative insights supported by modern science and astronomy. Stars contribute so much to the fertility and empowerment of all life-forms including our own life as Earthlings. Stars and stardust serve as rich metaphors for the Christmas birthing as explored in previous chapters.

Oh holy night, the stars are brightly shining
It is the night when stardust gives birth.
For aeons long, creation's unique splendour
As starlight shines upon our radiant shore.
A thrill of hope, for all that is begotten
For yonder breaks a new evolving dawn.

Chorus: Singing with joy — in grateful exultation,
The light shines forth — in cosmic radiating.
Oh Light, for all to see, O light! O light divine!

Led by the light, creation's evolution,
Stars in abundance inundate our space.

And life bursts forth amazing animation
As Earthlings sing in deeper gratitude.
With glowing hearts enlightening every nation,
May peace now reign in every human soul
Chorus: One Voice Unite ...

Truly God taught us to love one another;
At home in creation with care for our Earth.
With justice for all who share the resources
Befriending all life in our universe.
Let grace empower whatever now awakens
To bloom and grow in rich diversity.
Chorus: All sing with joy ...

3. Joy to the Earth! (Joy to the World)

I have already introduced this carol in Chapter One, a hymn based on Ps.98, written by the Englishman, Isaac Watts and first published in 1719. In the rewording below, I reframe the sense of our gratitude to God by more consciously adopting our call as Earthlings, embracing the challenge formulated by the scripture scholar John Dominic Crossan: "While we are waiting for God's intervention, God is actually waiting for our collaboration." (2010, pp 89-90).

Joy to the world, let earth rejoice! Let Earthlings raise one voice.
Resolving all division, and ending all dissension,
With peace on earth forever, and justice all will treasure,
And violence, and warfare, will be no more.

Joy to the Earth! Let justice reign! Let every hurt be healed.
Beyond all exploitation, and earthly degradation.
Let every creature nourish, and every life-form flourish,
And life, in fullness, will radiate.

Joy to all beings, the web of life, let every creature grow.
Let every species flourish, mid earth's abundant nourish.
What earth sustains in gratitude, for every season to include,
And fertile, our land, will long rejoice.

Joy to our God, Emmanuel, where Incarnation flows.
In all embodied creatures, and their evolving futures.
The energizing Spirit, empowering all for merit.
Re-echo, our song of joyful praise.

4. Music of the Spheres (Angels We Have Heard On High)

Based on a traditional French song, *Les Anges dans nos campagnes*, this carol was first published in 1843 and translated into English in 1862 by an English Catholic bishop, James Chadwick. It has been suggested that this spirited chant originated in a medieval Latin chorale when shepherds echoed across the hills of Southern France the joyous acclamation: "Gloria in excelsis Deo." The refrain echoed from hill to hill, spreading the celebratory news of Jesus' birth for the salvation of the world.

It is easy, and hopefully right, that we extend those joyful echoes beyond the merely human realm to embrace the planetary and cosmic dimensions of incarnation outlined throughout this book.

Music of the spheres on high, rhyme and rhythms of the sky.
And the earth in glad reply, echo forth its joyous cry:

Chorus: Gloria, in excelsis Deo! Gloria, in excelsis Deo!

Humans, why this jubilee? Cosmic strings the strain prolong!
What we see evolving here, all inspired by cosmic song? (Chorus).
Come this breakthrough celebrate, birthing forth as angels sing;
All creation God's decree, every creature praises ring. (Chorus).

Sacred space we celebrate, Bread of life, whom angels praise;
God of love is incarnate, And Earthlings blest our voice we raise.
(Chorus).

Chapter Five

The Wisdom of Archetypes, Our Hidden Resource

Only when the archetypal stratum is recovered does the story take on substance, dimensionality, life. Archetypal images act catalytically to transform. Walter Wink.

In this concluding chapter, I return to the notion of archetypes and their rich potential to liberate meaning, particularly in the spiritual realm — of both the person and the creation we inhabit. It is derived from two Greek words: *arche* denotes first or most basic, and *tupos* means type or form. Largely associated with the psychology of Carl G. Jung, archetypes are illustrations of what he called the *collective unconscious*, an envelope of creative energy from which everything in creation is begotten. The five primordial archetypes are Ether, Air, Fire, Water, and Earth. These foundational energies, either singularly or in combination, give rise to all other archetypes.

Many years ago, an American spiritual writer, William Bausch (1984, pp 70-71), offered this helpful explanation:

> That is why certain basic myths called archetypal keep popping up. Some are the sharing of food, denoting the sharing of the very substance that keeps one alive; hence the supreme value of hospitality, brotherhood, fellowship; the shedding of blood as a loss of vitality, and drinking it as drinking the source of life. There are Gods who died and rose again to explain the seasons. Miracles were used as proof of divine power. Virgin births were spoken of. The point is that these symbols are not unique to Christianity nor should they be. They are basic myths that explain humanity's eternal hopes, answers to the meaning of life, birth, death, tragedy, and suffering.

The following, therefore, are some of the key ingredients of archetypal wisdom. Parallels with quantum physics are immediately obvious:

- The archetype has no form of its own, but it acts as an "organising principle" on the things we see or do. It is a psychic power that draws mainly on intuition, imagination, and creativity from within.

- Rational logic in itself rarely opens us up to archetypal meaning. Imagination, intuition, and discerning wisdom are far more reliable resources. Dreams can be a valuable resource to make sense of archetypal images. But so can any form of artistic expression, from art, music, or poetry. Archetypal wisdom can also arise from meditation and deep reflection.

- In the archetypal realm, time is not the scientific notion of space-time. It deals with what we might call the eternal now. As John's Gospel suggests, such wisdom pre-exists the time frame of 2,000 years ago and continues to evolve into a fuller truth in our time and for the indefinite future.

- Particularly significant is the anthropological context, viewed in archetypal terms. As a species, we have evolved within an evolutionary story of some *seven million* years (more in O'Murchu 2008), an ancient sacred narrative that has been reduced and squeezed into the anthropocentric bottleneck of the age of civilization (approximately the past 5,000 years). This shrivelled anthropology has produced a number of cultural distortions, including central features of all the major religions. The current unease (disease?) around mainline religion may well be the result of our serious neglect of the archetypal realm.

- Is the archetypal merely a secular name for the divine? No! The archetype helps to illuminate the divine empowerment rising up from what Carl Jung called the collective unconscious, an ancient deep wisdom insinuated into creation at large.

Christmas as an Archetypal Season

The ubiquity of Christmas joy and celebration is a universal experience that defies rational explanation. Even for non-religious people, and in non-Christian cultures, it carries resonances that lure us in the direction of mystery and mystique. There is something in the Christmas season that exerts a universal appeal. Throughout this book, I name that enduring universal feature as the archetypal.

It seems, important therefore, that the Christmas Carols, while retaining the familiar and enduring melodies, adopt a language and horizon of meaning that honours this universality. Moreover, above and beyond the reformulations I offer in this book, I invite and encourage other people to create their own renderings. This can be an updating of Carols already well known, or attempts at ones that will be totally new — whatever the creativity in each person evokes.

To encourage and support such creative endeavours, I offer a final synthesis of the archetypal elements that characterise Christian faith as we understand it today.[10] And I illustrate some of

---

[10] This is the faith system with which I am most familiar, unique for those who call themselves Christian but not superior to other major religions. Accordingly, I

those elements by using poetry, a creative expression with which I am most familiar. For others that creative outlet might be art, sculpture, music, dance, gardening, etc. The archetypal works across all the creative arts and can be illuminated through them all.

Recovering Christianity's archetypes

For much of the past 2,000 years the Christian faith, like other world religions, has been focussed on *instinct* rather than on *archetype*. It offers a set of strategies for people to contain and control their instincts and through that process be better prepared to earn salvation in the afterlife. Such religion is concerned primarily if not exclusively with human beings, viewed as flawed creatures at the mercy of unruly instincts. Little or no attention is devoted to creation and its contribution to our growth and flourishing. Flawed humanity in a flawed creation has long been the underlying paradigm of mainline Christianity.

Look around the Christian world and one symbol stands out above all others, namely, *the Cross*, and typically bearing a tortured, crucified Jesus. The oldest historical evidence we have for this type of crucifix is that of the Gero Cross, housed in Cologne Cathedral in Germany and dated to 965 CE. Few Christians realise that the crucified image of Jesus on the Cross very much belongs to the

---

welcome and encourage people of other faith traditions to offer corresponding insights into their respective archetypal elements.

second Christian millennium and is inspired by St. Anselm's theory of Atonement, and not by the foundational message of Jesus and the Gospels, which see life rather than death as the pathway to holiness and salvation.

Much of the ensuing soteriology (theology of salvation) can be traced back to St. Paul, for whom the Gospel had predominantly one meaning: the death and resurrection of Jesus. Paul records nothing of the life of Jesus in terms of the Sermon on the Mount, the Parables, The Miracles, or the Infancy narratives. At one level, Paul does honour the primacy of the archetype over the instinct in this statement: "Where sin abounds, grace abounds all the more" (Rom.5:20). Unfortunately, the history of Christianity does not follow that vision.

What is mainly missing in Paul is the primacy for Jesus of what the Gospels describe as the Kingdom of God. I have already covered this topic in Chapter Two and explained my preferred renaming as the Companionship of Empowerment. This is the foundational archetype of the life and mission of Jesus, and as also indicated in Chapter Two, retained a significant influence on the development of Christianity up to the beginning of the 4th century when the Roman Emperor, Constantine, paved the way for making Christianity the official religion of the Empire. From there on imperial kingship, rather than empowering companionship, came to the fore. The instinct took preference to the archetype.

I want to offer some poetry to highlight the central role of this archetype in our Christian narrative. How Jesus sought to explain it and how his hearers might have heard his vision are captured in this poem below.

IMAGINE A NEW EMPOWERMENT

Imagine a Kingdom with no king at all,
Empowering companions in charge.
Imagine the seed, the smallest by far,
Producing a tree's entourage.
Imagine a farmer his wealth to forego
To purchase a treasure so rare.
A new dispensation explodes in our midst:
Imagine... Imagine... Imagine!
Imagine a vineyard with wine flowing profuse,
The joy of a new celebration.
Imagine a banquet with no one left out,
Disrupting the known segregation.
Imagine the sower with seedlings aglow,
A harvest to relish the nations.
No more malnutrition to torture the soul;
Imagine... Imagine... Imagine!
Imagine a woman with leaven and dough
The hands that make bread to sustain us.

Imagine a table that's open to all,

Where purity laws won't estrange us.

Imagine the workers for too long subdued,

The struggle for justice is reaping.

From the least to the greatest let everyone sing:

Imagine... Imagine... Imagine!

Imagine an end to the patriarch's reign,

Collapsing the power from on high.

Imagine a circle empowering within,

A freedom so new to employ.

Imagine the demons, controlling through fear,

No longer command the high ground.

A new world order can break through at last;

Imagine... Imagine... Imagine!

Imagine the challenge disciples embrace

To model the new dispensation.

The old bureaucratic with power at its core

Lies dead in the temple's ruination.

Imagine the courage and vision we need

When the tomb of our hopes has been shattered.

And the new voice arising has another refrain:

Imagine... Imagine... Imagine!

The Archetypal Jesus

The Kingdom of God, often described these days as the New Reign of God, had nothing at all to do with kings, kingships, and imperial dispensations. It seems that Jesus rejected entirely the God of imperial domination in favour of an upside-down-Kingdom, better named as the *Companionship of Empowerment*. The historical birth of Jesus, his formative years (from the little we know), and his call to mission, need to be reviewed within the context of this new companionship, marking the shift from instinct to archetype.

This will give us new insight into Jesus's relationship with John the Baptist, whose movement Jesus initially joined and later left, probably because of the ascetical flavour preoccupied with human instinct. As expressed by the American scripture scholar Thomas Sheehan (1986, 57), "Jesus' preaching was as riveting as John's, but different in tone and substance. Whereas John had emphasised the woes of impending judgement, Jesus preached the joy of God's immediate and liberating presence. A dirge had given way to a lyric." Once again poetry will release the shift towards the archetype:

PREPARE YE THE WAY OF THE LORD

> *The Baptist had them trembling with fear of things to come,*
> *The ashes and the sackcloth,*
> *The penance and the pain,*
> *The fearful hand of judgement*

What merit would they gain?

Apocalyptic vision — the frightening doom to come,
And the odds are stacked so heavy 'gainst those who would succumb.

Jesus joined the Baptist's rally, exploring future fate.
To seek his own vocation,
Excitement all around,
Awaiting the Messiah
The promised hopes abound.
But the people feel unworthy and are told they must repent
Lest they miss the golden moment of God's Messiah sent.

Jesus gazed upon the strategy and the Spirit led elsewhere.
He questioned the foundation
Of the fasting and the prayer
Envisioning alternatives
Of a strong prophetic flare.
Instead of disempowering those already colonized
He dreamt a new companionship with a dream to energise.

Jesus left aside the Baptist and chose another way.
The penance and the fasting,
The desert of the heart,
Instead let's dance in feasting
Set free and celebrate.
The powers were badly shaken, they could not comprehend

How people so transformed would throw caution to the wind.

For Jesus as an archetypal force, we encounter a new sense of God's presence to our lives and to our world. In Matthew's Gospel (1:23), Jesus is renamed as Emmanuel, which literally means God is with us. This divine presence, full of promise, life and hope, has been with us every step of the way since we first evolved seven million years ago. God's incarnation in our midst, the embodied solidarity of divine intimacy, is our grace and blessing. In archetypal terms it is a wholeness that is our divine birthright, one we must also embrace and make more real for all forms of embodied life. Never again must we restrict incarnation to the historical Jesus only.

INCARNATION: NEW HORIZONS

Why do we short-circuit the myst'ry we are,
Depleting our God-given glory,
Renouncing our deep ancient story,
And leaving us shrivelled mid echoes subduing!

Why do we deny the truth we now know,
The African prairies to roam,
And Earth is the place we call home,
Mid the millions of years we flourished anew!

Why are we so stuck in this civilized game,
Disparaging wisdom of old,
Creative allurement behold,
Long before false religion invaded our hope!

Why do we believe the theory we're flawed,
Insatiable hunger for power,
Organic connection gone sour,
We need to reclaim the subverted dream!

The dream is inscribed in birthing and dying
Of how we evolved mid millennial time.
And for most of that time as Earthlings endure,
We flourished and thrived in the Earth's fertile hue.

Earth's wisdom will save us, God's primary grace,
Reconnect with the Spirit, and follow its trace.

Finally, let us return to the metaphor that delivers the archetypal empowerment of our Christian faith and marks in a unique way our celebration of the Christmas time: *Birthing new life, hope, and meaning.* It is the dream and aspiration of every life-force to beget new life and to adorn creation with the richness and complexity amid which evolution flourishes. Every thought, every word, every gesture of love and compassion, every pregnant mother, and every fertile field — all mark the archetypal dynamic of our Birthing God! We rejoice and give thanks!

> *O Birthing God!*
> *Birth afresh in us the newness of an archetypal child,*
> *Awakening a vision wherein nothing is reviled.*
> *Yet, fragile and so tender,*
> *Exposed to every danger*
> *The living face of God on earth,*
> *Companion to us all.*
> *Birth afresh in us the flourishing of evolution's scope*
> *Enveloping the future, resilient in hope.*
> *The times may be uncertain.*
> *Many feel a sense of burden.*
> *But Emmanuel will lead us*
> *Companion to us all.*
> *Birth afresh in us the adult with evolution's thrust*
> *Engaging every challenge which comes to us robust.*
> *Beware the false allurement,*
> *The greed of power's procurement.*
> *Betray we not the face of God,*
> *Companion to us all.*
> *Birth afresh in us horizons of Incarnation's lure,*

The body of the earth our home, so gracious its inure.

Abundance is our blessed state

With justice we must ne'er negate

Reflecting faithfully God's face,

Companion to us all.

Birth afresh in us fidelity to God's New Reign on earth.

Companions for empowerment in every sphere give birth.

A New Reign of love and justice,

Undo every violent fortress.

The face of God that liberates,

Companion to us all.

References

Abrams, Nancy Ellen. 2015. *A God That Could be Real*. Boston: Beacon Press.

Armstrong, Karen. 2019. *The Lost Art of Scripture*. London: Vintage Books.

Bausch, William, 1984. *Storytelling: Imagination and Faith*. New London, CT: 23rd Publications.

Borg, Marcus & John D. Crossan. 2007. *The First Christmas*. San Francisco: Harper.

Boulter, Carmen. 1997. *Angels and Archetypes: An Evolutionary Map of Feminine Consciousness*. Rapid City, SD: Swan Raven & Co.

Carroll, James. 2014. *Christ Actually*. New York: Viking.

Crossan, John. D. 2007. *God and Empire*. New York: HarperOne.

    2010. *The Greatest Prayer*. New York: HarperCollins.

    2022. *Render Unto Caesar*. New York: HarperCollins.

Haight, Roger, 2019. *Faith and Evolution.* Maryknoll, NY: Orbis.

Haught, John F. 2010. *Making sense of Evolution.* Louisville, KY: Westminster/John Knox Press.

———. 2015. *Resting on the Future.* New York: Bloomsbury.

Hillmann, James. 1975. *Re-Visioning Psychology.* Washington, DC: Spring Publications.

———. 1983. *Archetypal Psychology.* Washington, DC: Spring Publications.

Howard-Brook, Wes. 2016. *Empire Baptized.* Maryknoll, NY: Orbis.

Levy, Paul. 2018. *The Quantum Revelation.* New York: Select Books.

Lieven, Dominic. 2022. *In the Shadow of the Gods.* London: Viking.

Kaku, Michio. 1999. *The Future of Humanity.* New York: Penguin Books.

Keenan, Peter, 2021. *The Birth of Jesus the Jew.* Dublin (Irl): Columba Books.

Keller, Catherine. 2003. *Face of the Deep.* New York: Routledge.

Johnson, Elizabeth. 2003. *Truly our Sister*. New York: Continuum.

———. 2014. *Ask the Beasts*. New York: Bloomsbury.

———. 2020. *Creation and the Cross*. Maryknoll, NY: Orbis.

Moore, Robert & Douglas Gillette. 1990. *King, Warrior, Magician, Lover*. New York: HarperCollins.

O'Murchu, Diarmuid. 2008. *Ancestral Grace*. Maryknoll, NY: Orbis.

———. 2011. *In the Beginning was the Spirit*. Maryknoll, NY: Orbis.

———. 2014. *On Being a Postcolonial Christian*. North Charleston, SC: CreateSpace.

———. 2017. *Incarnation*. Maryknoll, NY: Orbis.

———. 2019. *Doing Theology in an Evolutionary Way*. Maryknoll, NY: Orbis.

Rohr, Richard. 2019. *The Universal Christ*. New York: Convergent.

Schussler-Fiorenza, Elizabeth. 1992, *In Memory of Her*. London: SCM press.

Sheehan, Thomas. 1986. *The First Coming: How the Kingdom of God Became Christianity*. New York: Random House.

Stanford, Peter. 2022. *Angels: A Visible and Invisible History*. London: Hodder & Stoughton.

Swimme, Brian. 2022. *Cosmogenesis*. Berkeley, CA: Counterpoint.

Vearncombe, Erin & alia. 2022. *After Jesus Before Christianity*. New York: HarperOne.

Wink, Walter. 2002. *The Human Being: Jesus and the Enigma of the Son of Man*. Minneapolis: Augsburg Fortress.

Diarmuid O'Murchu is a priest and social psychologist, whose working life has been devoted to Adult Faith Development across much of the English-speaking world. His best known books include *Quantum Theology* (2004), *Adult Faith* (2010*)*, *In the Beginning was the Spirit* (2012), *When the Disciple Comes of Age* (2017); *Doing Theology in an Evolutionary Way* (2020), *Ecological Spirituality* (2024). Now as a retired missionary, he lives in Dublin, Ireland.

If you are interested in publishing, writing and you love to read, then head over to www.sleepylionpublishing.com

Otherwise, all questions can be sent to enquiries@sleepylionpublishing.com

If you would like to submit any work, whether a manuscript, short story, article, blog post or even artwork, then send us an email at submissions@sleepylionpublishing.com

We offer different paid contracts on smaller pieces, so whether you would rather an upfront payment, or to make money over time, we also personalize our collaborations. So, get in contact now and start earning money from your work!

https://www.facebook.com/sleepylionpublishing/

On our website you will find:

-Our personal editing, illustrating and publishing services and traditional royalty contracts

- Blog posts

-Articles on writing and reading

-Essays

-Short Stories

-Poetry

-And much, much more...

www.ingramcontent.com/pod-product-compliance
Lightning Source LLC
Chambersburg PA
CBHW050253120526
44590CB00016B/2339